# Hardys
# People

# Hardy's People

## FRANK HARDY

First published in 1986 by
Pascoe Publishing Pty Ltd
P.O. Box 51, Fairfield, Victoria, 3078
Australia

Printed in Australia by
The Dominion Press-Hedges and Bell
Maryborough, 3465
Typeset in Baskerville by Liz the Typesetter

© Frank Hardy 1986
HARDY'S PEOPLE
ISBN 0 947087 00 1

Book design by Stephen Pascoe

Illustrations by Moir

# CONTENTS

# The Most Australian Australian

When invited to attempt a column for People, I considered using the title "To Be Frank You Must Be Hardy".

That slogan was printed on a chimney in Port Melbourne by some genius of graffiti in 1951, during the criminal libel trial over the publication of my novel, *Power Without Glory*. (Until then I hadn't realised my name was really an apt play on words – and I didn't ever discover who invented that slogan.) Then Keith Dunstan, the Melbourne columnist, reminded me that Malcolm Muggeridge had called me "the most Australian Australian".

With the *Power Without Glory* television series being replayed on Channel 10 in Sydney, some know-all said to me in a pub the other day: "Carringbush is the original Aboriginal name for Collingwood."

So I had to explain.

I don't know what the Aboriginal name for Collingwood was. The genocidal activities against the Victorian Aboriginal probably created the situation in which nobody knows.

But I do know where the name Carringbush came from. In 1948, after two years of research, I began to write *Power Without Glory*. It was a novel, so I had to change the name of the suburb, Collingwood. I ran into trouble in the very first paragraph: "One bleak afternoon in the winter of 1893 a young man stood in the doorway of a shop in . . ."

I couldn't put Johnston Street, Collingwood, so I made some notes on a pad seeking an alternative.

In a flash of originality, I called Johnston Street, Jackson Street. But what to do with Collingwood?

It didn't take long to think of the idea of changing "wood" to "bush" then a bit of fiddling with the letters gave me Carringbush.

These words were provisional. They were too close to the originals; I'd alter them later.

More than one reviewer objected and, much later, Niall Brennan in his book *John Wren, Gambler*, launched a scorching attack on *Power Without Glory*, and one burden of his scorn was the unoriginal use of place names.

Thirty years later, there is a Carringbush library, and a Carringbush Hotel, and Collingwood barrackers sometimes sing "good old Carringbush for ever".

In 1980 I discovered that there was a horse called Carringbush. When I returned from France I headed straight for the Caulfield racetrack. A bookmaker challenged me: "I'll lay you a point over the odds on Carringbush."

I'd rather have a bet than a feed so I took 80 to 100 – and Carringbush bolted in.

It later won the Herbert Power Handicap, the Geelong Derby trial, and started favourite in the Melbourne Derby.

He was a great horse. Would have been a champion, except that he had only three and a half legs.

During my absence, a man named Billy Hope had named two of his horses after *Power Without Glory* (Carringbush has been retired to stud because of leg trouble, but Carringbush Lady is coming back into work and will win a race or two early in the new year).

I met Billy Hope by appointment at the Collingwood football ground. He is a tall, friendly man with a goatee beard.

"I once lived in Jackson Street, Carringbush," he said with a merry laugh. "So I told Ray Hutchins 'I had a special name that meant a lot to me. Find me a really good horse'."

A yearling by Cerreto, an Irish sire, who had won the Italian Derby, the colt showed them 23½ to the furlong and they called it Carringbush.

So, "what's in a name" as they say in the classics?

Well, it's a nice bloody feeling to have a name you invented pass into the language.

Just as well I didn't change the place names in *Power Without Glory* after all – but I wish to Christ (or Karl Marx) that I'd changed the name of the central character.

I omitted to say in court that John West was a composite-fictional character based on John Wren.

But sitting in the cell at the City Wash House one night, I felt that the closeness of the name made our defence difficult; and remembered that the very first time I wrote the name John West, on the very first page, I knew that I should have changed it. Four years later, I began to alter the name West to Smith on the 1700-page manuscript.

But I eventually gave up because the name appeared several times on every page – probably more than 10,000 times in all.

If only those egghead scientific bastards had invented the word processor at that time, I could have fed the name Smith into its memory bank.

Dear Citizens of Australia, it's a cruel, cruel world. I was finger-printed, jailed and put on a hit list – all because some stupid bastard was 30 years late inventing the computer. As Truthful Jones would say: "That's no bloody yarn!"

Which reminds me that I wrested the title of Australian Champion Spinner from tall-tale Tex Tyrell in 1966 – and I've just decided to give you the dubious pleasure of reading one of the yarns I used during that 11-hour epic battle in the Hotel Darwin.

# *Hardyarn*

I was locked in the vast corridors of the City Wash House Cell block when an old drunk was brought in and immediately went to sleep on the fingerprint table.

Waking some hours later he looked at me as though it were the first time he had ever seen a man in a neat blue suit with a collar and tie in jail.

He scratched his head and asked the first question asked in every jail on earth: "What are you in for?"

I hesitated. "For writing a book."

He gave his puzzled head a good long scratch then the light of understanding dawned in his roadmap eyes. "Ah, so you're a forger," he replied. "Been writin' crook cheques. I hope you beat the rap."

# Integrity Pays

There I am in the Billinudgel Hotel – one of the posher drinking holes on the fashionable North Coast – when who should I see at the other side of the bar but Truthful Jones himself.

Now, there are still people around who remember Truthful Jones. He used to contact me from all over Australia when I was telling yarns on the ABC TV series, Would You Believe?

Of course, Truthful is so named because he is the biggest liar in the southern hemisphere (but to say that to his face would be to risk a thumping).

Truthful and I welcome each other like long lost brothers which, in a way, we are – and we felt like a Tooheys or 10.

"Do you still bet on horses?" asks Truthful.

"I still bet like the Watsons," I tell him.

Now Truthful, being a student of linguistics and history, asks me an awkward question: "Who are the Watsons?"

So I ways to Truthful: "How the bloody hell would I know who the Watsons are. It's just a saying, like telling someone they are a bigger liar than Tom Pepper . . ."

Truthful gets a bit testy and asks if I am calling him a liar. Reassured by my purchasing him another schooner he says, thumbing his digger's hat on to the back of his head: "It just so happens that I know who the Watsons were: they were a rich family of pastoralists and every one of 'em ended up broke, after losing all their money on horses, dogs, lottery tickets, raffle tickets, poker machines, roulette – and flies crawling up the wall."

Truthful is one of those Australian battlers who can get you to believe him when he is pulling your leg; so, sensing some valuable Australian folklore, I asks: "What ever became of the Watson family?"

"About the others I don't know, but one of them,

nicknamed Integrity – because he didn't have any – went into the tipping business after he had lost one of the best farms in the Armidale district on the punt. Now, you might think it strange that a man who lost all his money punting could sell tips.

"Integrity Watson operated on the principle: Never give a sucker an even break. Integrity had a list of mugs who paid him to send them a telegram every Tuesday and Friday for the Wednesday and Saturday race meetings – and Integrity lived up to his name. One in eight of his clients got a winner at every meeting."

Foolishly, I asked how Integrity could be sure of this.

"Simple," Truthful replied. "He sent a different horse in a race with eight runners to eight different clients; one of them had to back a winner.

"This kept Integrity Watson in business for quite a few years, but eventually nearly all of his clients cancelled their subscriptions. Most of the mugs on the Mugs List stopped buying Integrity's tips. So one day Honest Herb Heffernan, Integrity Watson's partner, says: 'They wouldn't buy our tips if we sent a winner – after the race was over.'

"And this gives old Integrity the idea of the century. 'Herb, old mate,' he says, 'you're a genius.' Integrity gets caried away: 'Some of the mugs on our list would fall for it. I'll draft a telegram.' It read: 'Our special Saturday Hairylegs won five to one stop Forgot inform you stop As valuable client can now place bet after race stop Strict limit one hundred dollars stop Money order cash no cheques stop Integrity Investment Box 13 GPO.'

"If you don't believe me you can ask Integrity Watson. They invested their last money in 300 telegrams. And when they went to the Post Office they had to bring a suitcase to carry the letters away. The Most Generous Offer in History and the dream of every punter to back a winner after the race is over – 200 $100 letters in two days; 20,000 Oxford scholars. So up they choof to a travel agency and buy two one-way air tickets to the Bahamas."

Truthful Jones looks wistfully through the bar door at the serene green hills (as Patrick White would say) and shakes his head.

"Yer know, the human animal never quits while he is in front. Integrity and Honest Herb are in the pub having a last swig of Australian beer before they catch the plane, when Honest Herb says: 'It fair breaks me heart to think that over there in that box there's another bundle of letters just waiting to be picked up. Just one more trip across the road.' So over they go. Integrity's just about to put the key in the lock of Box 13 when three big detectives appear out of the gloom and charge them with fraud and conspiracy."

"They'd get a long stretch for a charge like that," says I.

"Integrity Watson was a bit of a bush lawyer," replies Truthful. "He conducts their defence. After the police and a few of the mugs gave evidence, he makes a speech: 'Your Honour, they don't call me Integrity Watson for nothing. We had every intention of paying these people at the odds of five to one, we were just ready to sign the cheques, but now that aspersions have been cast on our character, we are only going to refund their money'."

"Don't tell me they got off!" I says.

"Yeah, but they had to refund all the money though. Let that be a lesson to you, mate: there's no certainties in racing."

# *Hardyarn*

Truthful Jones definition of a mug punter: "The bloke who put his last $100 for the place on an odds-on favourite, it ran third, paid a money back dividend – and he lost the ticket."

# Liquor, Lyrics and Lawson

If a fellow named Niels Larsen hadn't arrived in Melbourne in 1856, heard about the Ballarat gold rush and consequently jumped ship, Banjo Patterson would be our national poet today. Larsen found no gold, he was even too late to fight in the Eureka Stockade, so he made his way to New South Wales, married Louisa Albury and their first-born was called Henry, Harry for short.

Now, there being the occasional racist in the district, as elsewhere in the colony, they decided while Henry was still a baby to anglicise their name to Lawson.

Henry, of course, went on to publish masterpieces like *Faces in the Street* and *His Father's Mate* before he was 20.

The mind boggles at the very idea of Larsen not jumping ship and not fathering Henry. Try to imagine an American tourist asking: "Who is your national poet?" You can't tell them it's Henry Lawson so you have to say Banjo Patterson. And your inquisitive American tourist would then ask: "Can you give me a few quotes from his poems?"

You'd feel bloody silly replying: "There was movement at the station for the word had passed around that the colt from Old Regret had got away" or "'Murder, bloody murder' cried the man from Ironbark."

To be fair to Banjo, some quotes from Henry mightn't go down too well with the Yanks either. Like:

If the people knew what the warders know
And felt what the prisoners feel
If the people knew they would storm their jails
As they stormed the old Bastille.

Or like:

"Would you have a moll to keep yer
And give up work for good?"
And the bastard from the bush replied,
"My bloody oath I would."

Or worse still:

> And so it will be, while the weary world goes round its
>   course
> The warning pen shall write in vain and the warning voice
>   grow hoarse,
> For not until a city feels Red Revolution's heat
> Will its sad people miss awhile the terrors of the street.
> The dreadful everlasting strife for scarcely clothes and
>   meat.
> In the pent track of the living dead, the city's cruel street.

Have you been around St Kilda or Kings Cross lately?
Lawson was writing about his Faces 100 years ago!

No offence to old Banjo, but Lawson would "play him on
a break" as a national poet. Come to think of it, I guess one
could understand why the academic critics knock Lawson
so much, just by reading the last of those quotations. They
feared his working-class, socialistic message and showed
their ignorance of art by criticising his literary style (Lawson
was, arguably, the greatest short story writer in the world at
the turn of the century and the greatest poet of rebellion,
into the bargain).

Of course, the old Harry hit back at his Establishment
critics in verses like:

> You were quick to pick on a faulty line
> That I tried to put my soul in
> Your eyes were keen for a dash of mine
> In place of a semi-colon
> But blind to the rest!
> You seek for truth in a language dead
> 'Neath tower and dome and steeple
> But what do you know of the tracks I've tread
> And what do you know of the people?
> I leave you alone in your cultured halls
> To drivel and croak and cavil
> Till your voices go farther than college walls
> Keep out of the tracks I travel.

Good on yer, Harry. Bore it up 'em!

The bastards are still at it to this day, almost 100 years
after Lawson began to write, so that he and the writers in his
realist, democratic tradition are taught to the sons and

15

daughters of suburbia in our universities as being mere journalists and propagandists.

If I really get warmed up on the subject of Uncle Harry Lawson I'll fill every page in this issue of *People*.

Actually, I only wrote this column to tell you a joke and to get in a free ad for a play I've written called *Who Was Harry Larsen?*

In this play I've tried to show how the identity and message of Lawson have been distorted to the detriment of the Australian people and nation.

Although Henry was a passionate, sometimes sad and even tragic figure, he had a marvellous sense of humour. He was strolling unsteadily up George Street one day when a woman, named Mary Someone, approached him to autograph a copy of one of his books she had in her handbag.

Henry inscribed: "Mary had a little lamb . . . And I had steak and onion".

# *Hardyarn*

Like most freelance writers in Australia, Henry Lawson often walked around with the arse out of his trousers. His mate, Victor Daley, also suffered often from "a touch of the shorts".

One day, in the '90s, they met in Pfahlet's Hotel near the old Bulletin office to discuss the deflationary trend in their currency.

They decided that the only way to "raise the wind" was for Victor Daley to go to the Bulletin office and tell the editor, Archibald, that Lawson was dead and he needed 50 quid for his funeral.

So Victor, a flamboyant Irishman with a red beard, headed off to the Bulletin office with the sad news, while Henry obtained a couple of free beers by writing a love poem to the barmaid.

Two hours went by, then three – and Victor had not returned. So Henry sat beside an empty glass sucking an empty pipe and he thought: "I'm rather on the deaf side; maybe Victor said that I should go and tell Archibald that he's dead."

So Henry toddled off down Margaret Street towards Archibald's office.

Meanwhile, Victor had, much earlier, walked up the stairs, knocked on Archibald's door and entered with a flourish and a suitably mournful expression.

Archibald (later famous because the Archibald Prize was named after him) was sitting at a small desk editing manuscripts and correcting proofs. He looked up and said: "Don't trouble me today, Victor, look at all this work."

Nothing loathe, Victor said: "I am the bearer of sad news." No reply from Archibald. So Victor had another go: "I bring the terrible tidings that Henry Lawson is dead and I need 50 quid for his funeral."

"Lawson dead? My God! We always leave it too late to try to understand people . . ." After more on the same theme, Archibald concluded: "I'll write an editorial on the red page: 'Vale Henry Lawson! The first genius of Australian Literature'."

"We'd better bury him first," Victor replied.

Archibald gave Victor a chit to the accountant for 50 pounds and laid his head in his arms on the table.

Archibald was still in this mournful posture when, three hours later, Henry Lawson stuck his head around the door and said: "Archie, I come as the bearer of sad news . . ."

Archibald looked up with teary eyes.

Lawson went on: "Victor Daley is . . ." The changed expression on Archibald's face warned Henry of the danger. "Victor's already been here . . ."

Henry Lawson beat a hasty retreat. Archibald threw a heavy inkwell at him, followed him down the stairs throwing books – and banned Henry and Victor from the Bulletin office for two years.

When Henry Lawson got back to the hotel, Victor had returned. He explained to Henry that he'd gone home to give his wife some of his share and pay off a bailiff who was waiting on the doorstep.

It's a true, funny but sad story.

Until I got this job with *People*, I often thought of pulling the same trick. Trouble was, I didn't know any editor who'd lend 50 quid to bury a writer.

# Lawson

I can't really remember when I chose to write a play on Henry Lawson's life. The theme probably chose me when, as a child, I heard my father recite Henry's poem *Faces In The Street*. It's opening line: "They lie the men who tell us, for reasons of their own, That want is here a stranger and that misery is unknown" haunted me when, as a teenager, I sought work in vain and knew and saw want and misery.

When I began to write, my first short stories were much influenced by Henry.

After the *Power Without Glory* trials (1950-51) I began to research Lawson's life in earnest, intending to write his biography. During the 30-odd years since, I have written hundreds of pages, in biographical and novel form.

Henry Lawson was such a complex man, his life so full of contradictions and secret layers, that the more you find out about him the less you feel you really know.

About 10 years ago, I took all I had written about Henry into Taffy's Restaurant, in Manly. It didn't read too bad but a reverential obsession forbade me to publish any of it until I really understood.

I vowed to rid myself of my obsession with the greatest of all the Australians, my Uncle Harry, as I had begun to call him.

But, little did I know!

Three people sitting at the other end of the restaurant told Taffy to ask me what I was writing about and to ask me to have a drink with them.

"Henry Lawson – and I'm not thirsty," was the stern reply – until they sent back word that they worked in Callan Park Mental Hospital and a patient in there believed he was Henry Lawson.

I visited "Henry Lawson" on several occasions. It was an

awe-inspiring experience to meet a man so obsessed with Lawson that he had taken over his identity; instead of pretending to be in his mental condition, Jesus Christ or Napoleon, he had, like a good Australian battler, chosen Henry Lawson.

I visited him several times (he has since died; I call him Ted Conway in the play – but that was not his actual name).

I would find him in one of three conditions: a man so interested in Lawson as to write slogans about him on the walls and on the slatted seats in the grounds; sitting in a corner saying nothing; or acting the role of Henry Lawson quite as well as Steven Tandy played young Harry Larsen up north.

One afternoon, when he was merely an admirer of Lawson, he was working with other inmates making pieces for jigsaw puzzles. We chatted – mainly about Henry Lawson.

At afternoon tea break, we stood in the queue, at the end of which another "loonie" was ladling out tea and coffee.

When we had placed our order, my new-found friend Ted Conway said to the tea server: "This is Frank Hardy, the author of *Power Without Glory*!"

The server replied: "Have they got him in here too?"

To this day I have never been able to fathom whether he meant that he wasn't surprised to find an inmate pretending to be me, or that he though it quite natural that I belonged in Callan Park. I think my play was born that day.

In March last year, I began to write it – and a year later it played to a packed first night audience at the Civic Centre, Murwillumbah.

I spent all last winter there, working on the play, at the invitation of an old friend, Virginia Catts.

The play was written in Murwillumbah – why not let it begin its journey around the world right there?

It's based on the life of Henry Lawson (Harry Larsen) with some new facts and insights; the main characters are Ted Conway, the mental hospital inmate who thinks he is Harry Larsen, and a writer obsessed with Larsen called Ross Franklyn, the pen-name I wrote under before *Power Without Glory*.

Some idea of the mixed-bag audience on opening night can be gleaned from the fact that Doug Anthony was sitting in the front row along with a representative of Neville Wran, Bob Debus, whose Cabinet post covers the Arts.

The former said (privately) that the play was good, not only for Murwillumbah but for the country. The latter said (publicly) that it succeeded because of, not in spite of, its radical content.

There were some tears and a lot of laughter and, it seemed to me, not a little rethinking of the real Australian traditions – and the response to Declan Affley and Helen Montgomery singing the musical settings by Chris Kempster of Lawson verses was wildly enthusiastic.

And, watching Steven Tandy (Tom in *The Sullivans*) playing young Larsen, and Leo Wockner playing the difficult dual role of old Harry Larsen and Ted Conway, my thoughts often turned to the man in Callan Park, who thought he was Henry Lawson.

# Moneyless Mugs

One of the Lawson poems Chris Dempster set to music recently for my play, *Who Was Harry Larsen?*, is called *One Hundred and Three*. It is a prison poem, a passionate cry against the "uselessly bad" conditions that prisoners suffer. There are some marvellous stanzas:

> The Champagne Lady comes home from the course led
>    in by the criminal swell,
> And they carry her in from the motor car to the lift of the
>    Grand Hotel.
> But armed with the savage Habituals Act they are waiting
>    for you and me,
> And drunkards in judgements on drunkards sit
> Keep step, One Hundred and Three.

The Habituals Act refers to the fact that Harry did a few stints under it for drunk and disorderly and resisting arrest. He was in jail quite often between 1905 and 1910, mainly for "wife starving", to wit, not paying maintenance.

On another occasion, he did a short stretch for obscene and abusive language. He happened to bump into a couple of ladies from Vaucluse. They threw some nasty, snobbish words at Uncle Henry, not knowing he was the most famous poet in the country. Nothing loathe, Lawson responded with some epithets which are unprintable. He ended up telling them that (and I leave out the swear words advisedly): "Your mink coats are stained with the blood and pain of animals, and the mansions you live in are built on factory toil and years of grinding rent. Your conscience is at peace but I am a better person than you – and *I'm* wanted by the police."

My favourite line from *One Hundred and Three* reads: "The clever scoundrels are all outside and the moneyless mugs in jail . . ."

The poem was written 65 years ago but that line remains

true to this day – most of the occupants of our prisons are moneyless mugs. A friend of mine, who must remain nameless, has a saying: "When you run out of money – only then do you get justice."

I wonder if Robert Trimbole would have "got justice" if some powerful figure behind the scene had not put up the hundreds of thousands of dollars the lawyers must have cost?

Trimbole, to my knowledge, is a bankrupt punter. But he is to be charged with serious crime, including conspiracy to murder.

A "moneyless mug" on far less serious charges would have been extradited and already in jail in Australia.

Of course, there are people who have committed serious and cruel crimes in our jails, but the majority are there, or waiting in the remand yards, for petty crimes, even for civil offences like being too poor to pay their debts or parking fines.

Indeed the clever scoundrels are all outside and are being protected by even cleverer scoundrels behind the scenes.

Who paid for Trimbole's defence? Who tipped him off to leave the country in a hurry when he was about to be arrested?

Where is Hand of the defunct Nugan Hand Bank? Frank Nugan committed suicide leaving, in his car, a "suicide note", in place of documents incriminating several respectable Australian citizens. These documents have never seen the light of day – but copies are in my possession.

You will remember, dear citizens of Australia, that Hand left the country as suddenly and mysteriously as Trimbole. Yet there is nothing in the newspapers about the manhunt which should have been mounted to bring him back.

Perhaps the powers that be don't want to find him.

One of the allegations against Trimbole is that he was involved in the conspiracy to kill the anti-drug crusader Donald Mackay.

Speaking as a moneyless mug who has twice been "sentenced to death" by killers hired by powerful interests, I have kept my eyes on this ominous hired killer syndrome.

I knew, and so did the NSW Police Force, who killed

Donald Mackay. I was powerless – the NSW Police chose to do nothing. Not until the man who arranged the killing crossed the Victorian border and was arrested by some straight Victorian cops were some of the conspirators brought to book.

Who killed Juanita Neilson?

She, like Donald Mackay, was a crusader against powerful business or criminal elements. Do the NSW Police know? And will one of the conspirators have to cross the Victorian border, if the crime is to be solved?

Most of the clever scoundrels are still outside.

# *Hardyarn*

Years ago a Sydney lawyer, named Not Guilty Nelson, began to specialise in defending bank employees who had "tickled the Peter".

His Little Mates in the legal profession wondered why he limited his considerable legal skills to this narrow field.

Little did they know.

A bank employee once approached Not Guilty and said he had stolen $40,000 from a certain institution that are "good sports with money."

"Could you steal another $60,000?" asked Not Guilty Nelson.

The bank clerk replied: "I probably could. It's easy when you've got the knack."

So Not Guilty Nelson said: "All right, go and steal another $60,000, give me $10,000 for my services, then I will ring up your employer and tell them the sad news."

The bank clerk asked: "What good would that do?"

Not Guilty Nelson replied impatiently: "I'll tell them you have confessed to me and that you are prepared to give back half of the money – and pay the rest off at so much per month.

"This way your employer avoids a scandal, gets back half of the money, plus so much a month. I get the honestly earned fee of 10,000 bucks – and you have already had the pleasure of spending your $40,000.

"What could be fairer than an offer like that?"

# Calling Commos, Crooks and Writers: Don't Go to Court

My father, Tom Hardy, used to say: "Never back odds-on favourites, never run up stairs – and never volunteer to go to court."

I did it once in my life – and let it be a warning to you, dear people who read *People*.

About 15 years ago a certain newspaper owned by a certain magnate published a story.

The story said I was one of those writers who joined the dole queue every year to get a financial grant from the Literature Board to assist me to carry out my literary work.

The truth was that I'd made only three applications in 30 years; one of 'em was knocked back, another succeeded for a few thousand bucks – and the third was vetoed by no less a person than Billy Snedden.

It was a funny set-up. The Literature Board made its recommendations and the leaders of the three political parties, Liberal, Labor and National Party (then known as the Country Party) rubber-stamped the recommendations.

On this occasion, however, Sir Billy, on behalf of the Liberal Party, said something like: "This is not on; we're not allowed to give grants to commos!"

Gough Whitlam, who was representing the Labor Party, said something like: "That's not correct; there is no such restriction!"

My wife, Rosslyn who was alive at the time (very much alive – and kicking!) said: "You ought to sue the so-and-so's Frank, that's a libel!"

I forget my father's advice, don't I? Never volunteer to go to court!

Now into the story comes no less a person than Athol George Mulley, the greatest jockey who ever threw a leg over a horse in this country.

The old Athol George had a column in another newspaper owned by the same magnate called *The Inside Running* and I was ghosting it for him.

We were getting 100 quid each and were underpaid at that.

Then this 'ere newspaper introduced computers, which, as you know, are the curse of the human race; but on this occasion a computer did us a good turn. Instead of sending me 100 quid and Athol George 100 quid every week, they sent us 200 quid each because some idiot (God bless him) had fed the wrong information into the newspaper's computer.

So we cop the extra 100 quid a week each and keep doing the column, until eventually someone checks the bloody computer and me and Athol George get sued for the money we'd been overpaid.

So I get a lawyer to write to this newspaper magnate and threaten to sue for libel for a bloody lot more money than they claimed me and Athol George owed 'em for writing the column (we were originally underpaid, anyway).

After some backin' and fillin' they settled out of court! They let me and Athold George keep the money we owed 'em and carry on regardless and they paid the costs.

Then bugger me if more than 10 years later the same newspaper owned by the same magnate publishes the same libel about muggins Hardy.

This time I'm in the dole queue every year, according to the journalist, lining up for me cheque from the Literature Board.

Now, in the meantime, I'd had one grant from the board so out of four applications in 35 years (many writers apply every bloody year) I'd received two grants, had one knocked back and the other vetoed.

So this time I sued the newspaper. Now I must mention a notorious letter written by Sir Robert Menzies, Ming the Bloody Merciless, many years before.

This letter said that no person who was or had been or was thinking of being a socialist or communist could get any dough from the Literature Board.

By the way, the reason for these grants is that book writers in this country earn on average about 4000 bucks a year.

So there I am in the Supreme Court, this time as a volunteer not as an unwilling victim as I'd been in courts in the past.

My plan and reason for taking out the libel case against this newspaper was to bring to light the Menzies letter.

It had been found by journalist Dick Hall and made public, exposing the fact that a veto had been applied to a grant from the Literature Board by Sir Billy. I had Gough Whitlam ready to go into court to swear on oath that the veto had been applied.

The case had taken two years to come on and meanwhile, Gough had gone to work for Unesco in Paris and couldn't get back for the case.

I was left without my star witness – and mention of the Menzies letter was ruled out of order.

So instead of a libel case in which I was the plaintiff I became the defendant in a court case cross-examined by none other dignitary than the now Justice McHugh, then a silk who spent a lot of time defending wealthy newspaper magnates against libel complaints.

I went into the box; the writer of the article did not! And I was there for two days, cross-examined by McHugh.

I gave as good as I received, won the battle with McHugh but lost the war in the eyes of the jury.

McHugh put me through hours of cross-examination about the *Power Without Glory* criminal libel trial of 1950-51.

I said at one stage that I was being re-tried on a charge on which a jury of 12 in Melbourne in 1951 had found me not guilty.

McHugh also spent several more hours cross-examining me on my political views.

Space does not permit quoting from the 200-odd pages of the transcript of evidence.

But at the end, my counsel and McHugh addressed the jury before the judge summed up.

McHugh told the jury I had been guilty in the *Power Without Glory* trial. He put to them as matters of fact, questions he'd asked me like: "Did you say in September 1963 . . ."

Not content with that, he put to the jury that I had portrayed in my comic novel *The Outcasts of Foolgarah* a certain lady of the realm fornicating in the bushes with a waiter.

No such scene appears in the novel.

So I go to the Appeals Court.

The jury had found "That the plaintiff is a hypocrite . . . and has been involved in attempts to establish a communist dictatorship in Australia."

The appeal took two years to come to court; and in the meantime who do you think was appointed judge of that court? Michael McHugh QC, that's who. He's now Justice McHugh of the Appeals Court of NSW.

Of course, Justice McHugh did not sit on my case.

The three judges who did (his fellow workers, so to speak) found that the jury's verdict was correct.

In other words, they used the Latin term for an old legal truism *capet lupinum*, which means head of the wolf.

A wolf may be hunted and killed and no one blamed and the old Frank Hardy cannot be defamed.

Never volunteer to go into a court. They're got up for judges, lawyers and policemen – and for the powerful of the land.

# *Hardyarn*

Once, when Athol George Mulley returned from riding in England, a journalist asked him if he had struck many heavy tracks over there.

"Heavy tracks?" he replied. "One day, I was trotting around to the start of a race when I saw a jockey's cap on the track. I leaned out of the saddle to pick it up.

"Just as I grabbed the cap, I heard a voice say: 'Don't pull until I get me feet out of the stirrups'."

# Life's a Lotto Worries

Australians, says Truthful Jones, are the greatest race of worriers since the fall of the Aztecs. Truthful was sitting in the bar of the Billinudgel Hotel, where all the posh people and yahoos hang out up the North Coast.

"How do you make that out?" I asked, buying another round of drinks. "Your average Australian laughs a lot."

"He's laughin' and can't afford it," replied Truthful. "The Australian laughs to hide his worries. The sad clown, so to speak."

I decided not to interrupt again; when Truthful is in full flight on a promising theme you don't interrupt him – except to buy a drink.

Well (Truthful Jones continued) there was this fella who couldn't stop worrying. He worked overtime at it. The lowest paid clerk in the biggest office in Martin Place. Worried when he couldn't balance the stamp money; worried when it balanced, because he must have made a mistake. Worried he might get the sack; worried he might get into a rut if he stayed in the job too long. Worried because he had no children; then worried that he might have children and not be able to bring them up right. Worried that his wife might be unfaithful to him; and worried that she must be a dull woman when other men took no interest in her. Worried because he thought people were talking about him; and worried because people weren't interested in him.

(I bought another beer – and Truthful took a big gulp of his without missing a word.)

He had an anxiety complex so big that Winterset couldn't have jumped over it.

If he ever stopped worrying, he worried because he had nothing to worry about. It got so bad his wife started worrying because he was worried; and he started worrying about his wife being worried. Then he started worrying about the nuclear threat – and that really sent him around the bend. So he went to one of those shrinks. Then he started worrying about how he'd pay the psychiatrist's bills. Then a funny thing happened: he won the bloody Lotto!

I bought another drink and commented: "And at last he stopped worrying."

Not him (Truthful Jones proceeded), he started to worry what to do with the money. Lay awake at night thinking people would touch him for it. Well, one day one of his mates at work, a bit of a hard case, said: "What are you worrying about? You've got plenty of money; why don't you employ someone to do your worrying for you?" So he puts an advert in the paper. *Worrier required. Only experienced men need apply. Excellent salary.*

And he got one reply. A little skinny fella with worry lines all over his face and haunted eyes. Had good references, too. Been bankrupt twice. Married twice and both his wives left him, which worried him a lot for some reason. A bigger worrier than his new employer, if that was possible.

Of course, the world's worst worrier had to make sure he had the right man. He was going to pay big money. He asked him a lot of questions, but he couldn't fault him. At last he asked: "Do you bite your fingernails, like me?" And the applicant replied: "I'm such a worrier, I bite other people's fingernails."

Well that clinched it. He gave him the job and stopped worrying on the spot.

Then he took his wife for a trip to the Barrier Reef. He never worried. Always bright and cheerful. Stopped biting his fingernails.

Made his wife the happiest woman in Australia. If he got a worry he just referred it to the professional worrier. He became the most happy-go-lucky man in the world.

One day his wife said to him: "I hate to worry you dear but the bank manager's just rung up and, because you're paying that man so much to do your worrying, all your money's gone and you're in debt."

Truthful Jones studied his empty glass and gazed through the door at the banana-coloured sunset (as Patrick White would have said) and delivered the punch line: "No use tellin' me that," the world's worst worrier replied. "That's his bloody worry."

# Hardyarn

Now, Truthful Jones has a yarn-spinning trick of inventing Smart-Alec definitions.

He delivered one before closing time that night at the Billinudgel pub.

Truthful Jones' definition of a real mate: A Catholic who gives up doing good turns for Lent.

# The World's Worst Whinger

There I was, drinking with Truthful Jones in the Billinudgel Hotel up the NSW North Coast.

Truthful appeared to have run out of yarns but I bought him a beer nevertheless and asked: "Would these yarns you tell be peculiarly Australian, or would there be variants of them in other countries?"

Truthful Jones sipped his beer and replied: "My yarns are all true . . . well, put it this way: every yarn is true to the yarnspinner who's telling it."

"I once heard a couple of your yarns in London," I told Truthful.

"They must have spread there by word of mouth," Truthful replied.

"What would be the best Australian story you ever heard?" I persisted.

"Well," Truthful replied reflectively, "I reckon the most fair dinkum Australian story ever told is the one about the great Australian Whinger . . ."

"I've hard of the whingeing Pom – but never the whingeing Australian . . ."

"The worst whinger was an Australian. I first met him – the World's Worst Whinger – in a shearing shed in Queensland during the Depression. I asked him an innocent question: 'How would you be?'

"Well, he dropped the sheep he was shearing, spat, fixed me with a pair of bitter eyes and says: 'How would I be? How would you expect me to be? Get a load of me, will yer? Dags on every inch of me hide; drinkin' me own sweat; swallowing dirt with every breath I breathe; shearing sheep that should 'ave been dogs' meat years ago; working for the lousiest boss in Australia; frightened to leave because the old woman's lookin' for me in Brisbane with a maintenance order. How would I be? I haven't tasted beer for weeks and

the last glass I had was knocked over by some clumsy coot before I finished it!'"

"He must have been a whinger, all right," I said

"The world's worst, like I told you. Next time I met him he was in an army camp in Melbourne. He'd joined the AIF. 'How would you be?' I asked him.

"'How would I be? Get a load of this outfit. Look at me flamin' hat. Size nine and a half and I take six and a half. Get and eyeful of these strides – you could hide a blasted brewery horse in the seat of them and still 'ave room for me. And get on to these boots, will yer? There's enough leather in 'em to make a full set of harness. And some idiot brasshat told me this was a man's outfit. How would I be? How would you expect me to be?'"

"Is this story true?" I asked.

"Well, most of my stories are true, but this one, you might say, is truer than true! I met him next in Tobruk. He was sitting on a box, tin hat over one eye, cigarette butt dangling from his bottom lip, rifle leaning on one knee, cleaning his fingernails with the bayonet.

"I should have known better, but I asked: 'How would you be?' He swallowed his cigarette butt and stared at me with a malevolent eye. 'How would I be? How would you expect me to be? Shot at by every Fritz in Africa; eating sand with every meal; flies in me eyes; frightened to go to sleep expecting to die in this God-forsaken place. And you ask me HOW WOULD I BE?'"

"Did you ever meet him again?"

"No, he was killed at Tobruk as a matter of fact."

"Well, one thing, he wouldn't do any more whingeing, poor devil."

"You know," said Truthful, "I dreamt about him the other night. I dreamt I died and went to Heaven. It was as clear as on a television screen. I saw him there in my dream and I asked: 'How would you be, mate?'

"He eyed me with an angelic expression and he says: 'How would I be? Get an eyeful of this nightgown, will yer? A man trips over it 50 times a day and takes 10 minutes to lift it to scratch his knee.

"'And take a gander at me right wing, feathers falling out of it – a man must be moulting. Cast yer eye over this halo; only me big ears keep the rotten thing on me skull. And just take a Captain Cook at this harp – five strings missing and there's band practice in five minutes! HOW WOULD I BE? HOW WOULD YOU EXPECT A MAN TO BLOODY WELL BE???'"

"A good story," I admitted. "Yes, a beauty."

"The most fair dinkum Australian story ever told," Truthful Jones replied, downing the last of his beer.

# *Hardyarn*

The difference between a whinger and a genuinely unlucky man is that your whinger would complain in heaven, whereas your unlucky man would, if it were raining mansions, get hit on the head with a Ferntree Gully dunny.

The unluckiest man in the world, according to Truthful Jones, was Hard Luck Harry Hardiman.

Hard Luck Harry bought a suit with two pairs of trousers – and burned a hole in the jacket. He backed a galloper in the last race one day at Moonee Valley – each way in a field of eight. It ran third in the first race at the trots that night.

In desperation Harry took up kidnapping. He kidnapped an orphan – and had to put it through university.

# *They* are the Trouble!

Truthful Jones emptied his glass and said reflectively: "You were probably right when you said to the people who read *People* that the basis of Australian humour is you can't win but you've got to battle. . . ."

I ordered two more beers and nibbled on a Billinudgel pie. "I thought you would agree; most of your stories are about battlers."

"Yeh," said Truthful, grabbing his glass in his great right hand. "But the question is, who do the battlers battle against?"

He had me there. "That's a good question . . . the government? . . . the system? . . ."

"*They!*" Truthful replied. "That's who we have to battle against."

"*They?*"

"They! Those bastards up there who won't give the battler a fair go."

"Who are they?" I asked, and lined up another drink so as not to interrupt Truthful's flow.

"I've been trying to find out who they are for years – and I'm still working on it. Take the races. In Brisbane a few weeks ago, I was going to back Lord Ballina, see, and a fella comes up to me for no reason at all – I'd never seen him before in my life – yet he comes up and says: 'They tell me Princess Tiber can't get beat. Just a matter of how far, they say.'

"So I says: 'They do, do they? I'd better back it then.' Needless to say, Lord Ballina beat Princess Tiber. So I see this character at the bar, see, so I goes over and says: 'I thought you said *they* said Princes Tiber couldn't get beat.'

"'So they did,' he says. 'And who were *they?*' I asks. And he didn't know who *they* were either. And he says to me: 'I'm sorry mate, but it was *their* fault. *They* are the trouble.'"

I said to Truthful: "*They* are the trouble. A good theme, that."

"They've got a lot to answer for, all right," Truthful continued. "They throw heads when you back tails at the two-up. They run their horses dead. They rob you in the Parliament. They charge high rent. They start depressions. They cause wars. What they do is bad enough but why can't they ever learn?"

"They'll never learn. They wouldn't wake up if an Adelaide River dunny fell on 'em. They wouldn't know horse dung from clay unless they tasted it. They can't see any further than their noses.

"They're sending the country broke. They say we've never had it so good. They say there's no such thing as a free lunch – but they eat one nearly every day. They won't give a man a fair go. They sell the country out to the Yanks. They couldn't run a raffle, mate, that's for sure."

"They say it's a good idea to drown your sorrows," I quipped, "so you'd better have another beer."

"They wouldn't know, mate. But I'll force one down just to be sociable. They start a lot of gossip, too. They say he married her for her money. They say she had to get married. They say their marriage is on the rocks. They say he's a bad pay. They say she's a smack addict."

I warmed to Truthful's theme. "What about the Tax Summit. Were *they* behind that?"

"No worries. They and no other. Keating promised to become Robin Hood and tax the rich and give it to the poor. Instead he became a dray driver and robbed the poor and gave it to the rich."

I asked: "Did they build the cart for him?"

Truthful replied: "They did indeed but they're lousy carpenters. Trouble is: they've got other options. When the wheel came off the cart, they made a deal with Keating and Hawke for a worse package than Option C."

Truthful Jones sighed, tipped his hat back with his thumb and gazed at the surrounding green-wooded hills of the Tweed Valley. "They are the trouble, all right. . ."

I sighed and lit my pipe. "I wish we could find out who they are."

"If wishes were Mercedes, beggars would ride in style,"
Truthful replied. 'Next time someone sidles up to me and
says: 'They tell me the Opera House is going to be raffled,'
I'll say: 'And who are *they*?'"

"Trouble is they won't know who *they* are," I ventured.

"There you go, trying to spoil my story again. My father
always said: 'They will try to make you get ahead of your
story, but don't let them.' Every time anyone says: 'They say
. . . ' I'll demand to know who *they* are."

"But they won't tell you," I chiacked him.

"Or maybe they wouldn't even know, as you say. But I'll
work on it until I find out who they are. I've made up my
mind to kill the lot of them."

"Good idea," I said. "Have another beer before *they* close
the pub."

"Yeh, they've got it coming to them. They'll get theirs and
the world will be a better place with them not in it," Truthful
asserted.

"Yeh, they say we'd be better off without them."

"How would they know?" Truthful replied, then did a
double take. "How come they are so powerful – if they don't
know?"

"Perhaps they are born to it," I suggested. "With silver
spoons in their mouths. Inherited money. . ."

"Or maybe they started work with the public service or
the finance companies at an early age and were trained in
bastardry," Truthful replied and thumped the bar with his
fist. "Anyway, *they* can all get well stuffed for mine!"

# Hardyarn

Truthful Jones' definition of THEY.

"They are toffs and silvertails who never did an honest
day's work in their lives – and think Manual Labour is a
Spanish Bullfighter."

# The Needy and the Greedy

Years ago while writing a novel I paid my rent by ghosting a newspaper column, *The Inside Running*, for Athol George Mulley.

For the uninitiated, he was arguably the greatest jockey who ever rode on an Australian racecourse. He rode the mighty Bernborough for 15 consecutive wins, a world record to this day.

Mulley reckoned Bernborough was so intelligent he bowed to the crowd after every victory and learned how to talk. At the track one morning, Bernborough said to another horse, "I can't remember your mane but your pace is familiar." Ugh!

We first met soon after the publication of my novel *The Four-Legged Lottery*, the title of which came from Egon Kisch's remark: "Horse racing, in Australia, is a lottery with four-legged tickets."

The book had an anti-gambling theme, and I was surprised to find that this was one of the reasons Mulley liked it.

One day, as we entered Randwick race-course, Athol George surveyed the punters streaming in and said: "There they go: the needy and the greedy."

He had summed up the Aussie punter – and the needy are in the vast majority.

Athol George arrived at Kembla Grange racecourse. A battling trainer approached him: "Will you ride my horse in the maiden handicap?" Mulley replied: "Sorry, I'm here for one mount. Anyway, your horse has raced a dozen times without winning."

The trainer persisted: "Between you and me, it's won three maiden handicaps under different names – its real name is Fine Thread."

Mulley was the jockey punters loved to hate. One day, he

rode the first five winners at Canterbury, and when he got beaten on the favourite in the sixth, the punters booed and threw race books and pie crusts at him.

Athol George took it as a part of the game – and told a story against himself on the theme. An Irish punter was in the pub Saturday morning studying the racing form. His mate rushed in and yelled: "Hey, Pat, they reckon the Pope's dead!" The Irishman replied: "I'll bet that bastard Mulley is riding it."

Athol George reckoned all punters were superstitious. One said his lucky number was eight. On August eight at Flemington races, he saw in his race book a horse in race eight which had number eight at the barrier and had run eighth at its last start. So, naturally, he had $8 on it. The horse ran eighth and he had to borrow $8 for his taxi fare home.

The late Stan Fox, millionaire racehorse owner, was driving his car out of the car park at Rosehill races when a "desperate" hailed him. "How did you get to the races?" Stan Fox asked.

"On the train," was the reply.

When the battler got in, Stan asked him: "Why didn't you get a train home?"

"I only bought a single ticket; didn't want to ruin me bank," the battler replied. "I haven't got a cent left. I'm the most desperate gambler in Sydney."

Stan Fox, who didn't approve of other people gambling, gave the punter quite a lecture on the evils of gambling.

"I'm a millionaire. I own 50 horses, have a private trainer and Athol Mulley rides all my horses, yet I can't win gambling," Stan rattled on. "What hope would a mug like you have? How much do you earn a week?"

The battler replied that he earned only about $250 and that he had a wife and two kids.

Stan Fox took pity on him and gave him $100: "Here, take that home to your wife and promise me you will never gamble again."

The battler crossed his heart and promised faithfully and they shook hands when Stan dropped him off.

But lo and behold, a few weeks later, Stan Fox was driving out of Randwick race course when the same desperate hailed him for a lift again and admitted he was stoney-broke, having lost all his wages at the race meeting.

Stan Fox did his block but relented and gave the punter $100 on the promise that he would never ever back a racehorse again as long as he lived.

But the very next week, Stan Fox again saw him waiting for a lift outside the race course. Stan was furious but pulled up.

"I'm not taking a lift from you," the battler said. "You bring me bad luck. Every time you give me a lift, I do me money."

Attendances at horse racing have fallen away steeply lately. The main reason is that the TAB has modernised its facilities and spread its net to bet on between 50 and 70 races every day, (some run in towns you wouldn't find on a map) six days a week to trap the needy.

The percentages it takes to meet top-heavy administration costs and the millions it rips off for the government makes the punter's task impossible.

Last time I met Mulley, I said, "Not many people going to the races these days."

"No," Mulley replied, "the needy are betting on the TAB. And that reminds me of a yarn.

"One Saturday morning, a character rang the Moonee Valley Racing Club from Shepparton. 'I'm bringing a busload of people down to the races,' he said. 'What time is the first race?'

"'What time can you get here?' replied the man from the MVRC."

If Athol George Mulley had been a contestant when I won the Australian Yarn-Spinning Championship in that epic battle with Tall-Tale Tex Tyrrell, he might have beat me in a photo finish.

# *Hardyarn*

Mulley rode with success in France for the famous owner, Madame Mareotti.

When he returned to Australia, racing commentator Des Hoysted interviewed him on the radio.

"Did you eat any snails in Paris?"

The old Athol George replied: "No, but I rode quite a few."

# George's Ploys: from Toys to Spies-in-the-sky

My father used to sing an old Wobbly song – its chorus went something like this: "Work all day, live on hay, there'll be pie in the sky when you die."

Now, in NSW at least, it's a case of spy-in-the-sky.

George Paciullo, the new police minister, has announced that speed not booze is the main killer on the roads and he proposes to introduce a helicopter equipped with radar to fly above the highways and country roads to catch speeding motorists.

The Wran government has got some terrific ministers. The old Nifty reshuffled his cabinet to share the brilliance between departments. For example, he switched George from consumer affairs to police.

George did a terrific job. When you look up consumer affairs in NSW the first extension on the list is general complaints and the second is consumer affairs enquiries.

When you ask for the complaints section for example, it's engaged.

It's just as bad in Victoria. A couple of years ago I rang up consumer affairs every 10 minutes for two days. And eventually I got on. I put on a big act and I told the bloke who answered the phone I was gonna complain to the minister.

As consumer affairs minister George Paciullo achieved two great things that will cause him to go down in history.

He and his department revised the hire purchase time payment laws and instead of hiring a car or a television set under a hire purchase agreement you actually got one under a mortgage agreement and people thought hooray!

There are new credit laws and the finance companies are going to get hell from George.

Well, as it turned out, the new legislation helped the finance companies and the Retail Traders Association and their debt collectors.

Under the old law, everyone who entered your house to settle a debt was acting illegally.

But under the new legislation the old George legalised repossession, so that if your car's in the garage they can grab it. They can also come into your house, after getting a court order, and seize the goods if you're a bit behind in your payments. And who isn't these days?

Having really fixed up the new credit laws, George then brought in what he cleverly called a new "managerial strategy in consumer affairs."

Now, do I hear some of the people who read *People* ask: "Where the hell did you get this inside information about the consumer affairs department? From Truthful Jones?"

Well, not directly from Truthful.

There I was sitting in the Harold Park Hotel, when who should walk in but Truthful and this thick-set fella with a round, smiling, cunning face.

So I says to Truthful: "Who's your mate?"

When the smiling fat fella went to the bar to buy some drinks, Truthful says: "Don't knock him, I picked him up on the way down from Alice Springs."

"He's a fountain of bloody information on every subject on earth. They call him Chinese Jack."

So Chinese Jack comes back and I tell him I'm trying to gather some information on the consumer affairs department and he says: "That ain't no consumer affairs department any more.

"The old George didn't want any bloody complaints, so the phone's engaged all the time, and if you get so far as getting a complaint in, you sit down with the finance company of the traders, and members of his staff, acting as what he calls honest brokers."

I says to Chinese Jack: "Where did you get all this information, how do you know?"

Truthful interjected: "Because he's the greatest bloody moaner and complainer in the southern hemisphere and has never knocked off in the last three years sending in complaints to the consumer affairs department.

"Before he went to Central Australia, he used to go in there nearly every day and hang about until someone saw him. So they gave him a file and he's made tapes."

My rather low opinion of this tubby little grinning Chinese chap changes quick and smart doesn't it?

'Specially when he says with a sly grin: "You can understand Paciullo and his staff taking this attitude.

"I mean how are they going to get on with their work in there, making all them films and puttin' out all them leaflets and PR pamphlets and other bullshit – how are they gonna get on with all that work if the public keeps ringin' up and comin' in and complainin'?"

So Truthful slaps me on the back and I go and buy a drink.

Then Chinese Jack says: "I'm with Truthful in the jeep, see? and I says to Truthful, 'We've been followed by a flying saucer.'

"And Truthful says: 'It's not a flying saucer, it's a bloody helicopter!'

"If it's a helicopter, it's flying along behind us', and the next thing we get pulled over by the bloody coppers."

Truthful took up the story. "I says to this policeman: 'How do you know we were over the speed limit, you were in front of us, not behind us.'

"The policeman replies: 'The-spy-in-the-sky. There's a radar in that helicopter up there and they caught you doing 140 – and I'm bookin' ya'."

Chinese Jack buys another drink: "And they can repossess on short notice and they can evict people for not being able to afford to pay their rent on 24 hours' notice, and now they can catch you for speeding with a spy-in-the-sky."

"How do you explain a brilliant man like George doin' such a great job in two successive portfolios?" I asked no one in particular.

Chinese Jack replies: "He's a gimmick man. While he was working overtime to stop the consumers complaining to the consumer affairs department, he had the gimmick of killer toys, remember?"

Truthful Jones comments quietly: 'I wonder what he's really up to now while he's keeping our attention on the gimmick of the spy-in-the-sky?"

Chinese Jack grins slyer than ever: "Ah, he'd be workin' on a new management strategy for the police force."

# *Hardyarn*

Years ago, I went to Randwick races with Truthful Jones. We managed to back a winner and Truthful went off to buy two pies to celebrate the rare occasion. We take our pies to the lawn in front of the bar to watch the next race.

We're each holding our pie delicately with the sauce running down the back of our hand and the juice running down the front. We're eatin' away at these beautiful pies when someone behind me bumps me elbow and me pie goes crashing to the ground.

I turn like a flash: "You awkward bastard! Look what you've done! Fouled-up me beautiful pie!"

And I look up, and I look up higher, and there's about the biggest bloody policeman I've ever seen in me life.

And there's Truthful grinnin' away to himself: "Hardy's going to be dragged off to the lock-up just once more."

Now, you'd better believe this: this policeman sees the funny side and he starts to laugh, and I laugh with relief, and Truthful laughs.

And there the three of us are, standing on the lawn at Randwick laughing our heads off.

Truthful Jones has often said since that I'm the only man in the history of Australia who called a policeman a bastard and the copper burst out laughing.

# Hollywood Ten – Melbourne One

The early '50s was the time of McCarthyism, the use of the Red bogey (the Communist Party Dissolution Act which found no Reds under the bed) and the Petrov Spy Commission which found no spies under the carpet.

I couldn't have picked a worse time to publish my first novel, exposing the corruption of the system. I was dragged from obscurity onto the front pages, into jail and the dock of the Supreme Court (criminal jurisdiction).

A cheeky mug from my earliest years, I had insisted on being arrested By Appointment Only. When two members of the Special Branch, O'Connor and Moody, came looking for me I went into hiding for a few days and my wife and children went bush. Then I rang Russell Street police headquarters and told the Commissioner I could be arrested in the office of Thomas Dall, solicitor, at three o'clock.

O'Connor and Moody turned up on time. I believed I was going to be arrested for theft. My mate, George Seelaf, had had the second edition of *Power Without Glory* run off in a printery, owned by John Wren himself, secretly on the nightshift. Wren's cohorts had discovered our subterfuge, put a police guard on the premises overnight, intending to burn the offending material next morning.

Seelaf and I, acting on our theory of controlled audacity, "robbed" the place of our printed and partly folded pages, taking the laudable precaution of stealing a tonne of paper on which to print the third edition.

Imagine the scene in Tom Dall's office. The honest lawyer looking a bit out of his depth and yours truly mirroring what Henry Lawson called the "terrible look of the caught"; Detective Sergeant O'Connor looking sleek and sinister in a flash grey suit and Detective Moody looking flabby and foolish in a chair that threatened to collapse under him.

O'Connor produced a piece of blue paper and began to read the indictment. "You have committed a criminal and seditious libel (what the hell's that?) in that you did publish and cause to be published a document known as *Power Without Glory* in which you stated that Mrs Ellen Wren entered into an adulterous relationship with a bricklayer and bore a child by him."

He then proceeded to read the sections of the novel about the love afair between Nellie West and Bill Evans.

Every time the name Nellie was mentioned O'Connor paused, looked at me and said: "Meaning thereby the informant". For example: "Nellie (meaning thereby the informant) kissed him passionately."

Eventually, I began to laugh every time he said: "Meaning thereby the informant."

The laugh was on the other side of my face when the cops drove me to the City Watch-house, emptied my pockets and took my fingerprints.

So I became one of the main victims of Australian McCarthyism.

In America, Senator McCarthy had dragged communist writers and actors before the Un-American Activities Committee. They were jailed for contempt and blacklisted from their profession. They became known as the Hollywood Ten.

Many years later, a French journal carried an article about me called *The Melbourne One*. I was proud of that; I've always wanted to be counted where I belong – on the side of the battlers of our society.

My reaction to the arrest and the nine months of court cases and campaigning was typically Australian: I found it comical as well as tragic.

Seelaf, in an interview with *Four Corners* 25 years later, when *Power Without Glory* went on television, was asked how he remembered me at the time. He replied: "Well, he laughed a lot."

I was isolated and excluded from the media after the trial was over. But I didn't give a stuff and was much heartened by the irony of Malcom Muggeridge calling me, in 1958, "the most Australian of all the Australians."

My love of this country differs from that of the jingo patriots who fall about when a millionaire wins a yacht race. My pride arises from the character and attitudes of the ordinary people: "You can't win, you've got to battle; give the battler a fair go."

The jury eventually acquitted me and 25 years later *Power Without Glory* went on television. I came to the conclusion that this strange turn of the wheel of history was as much a compliment to the basically rebellious spirit of the Australian battler which insists on a fair go, as to any contribution I might have made.

When a victim of McCarthyism eventually becomes the "most Australian Australian", one realises that it could only have happened in this country.

And I pondered again on this matter when Kerry Packer cried: "McCarthyism" during and after the Costigan Royal Commission and his sentiments were echoed by Bob Hawke and Neville Wran.

Beware, dear citizens of Australia, when a multi-millionaire and two right-wing politicians cry McCarthyism, when an honest Royal Commissioner dares to question the reason why $1 million is drawn out of a bank in cash and one millionaire lends another a quarter of a million, interest free and without a receipt, and the reason given was that Kerry had a squirrel mentality and likes the occasional punt on a horse. Beware, for you live in a land of the double standard where words have lost their meaning.

Kerry Packer was a "victim" of Costiganism – and to equate Costigan with McCarthy is like comparing a nun with a madam of a brothel.

McCarthyism was mindless, bigoted, anti-communism aimed at striking fear into the hearts of liberal and radical-minded people who believed there must be an alternative to the dog-eat-dog philosophy of capitalism.

Costiganism, on the other hand, means an honest Royal Commissioner investigating organised crime and not backing off when some of the trials led to rich and powerful men. And I'm sure the Australian battler will not have a bar of the bleatings of "McCarthyism" in a situation which is its very opposite.

In the McCarthy period, the victims were "donkeys" like me and Big Jim Healy (no offence, God rest his soul). Under Costiganism the victims are goannas. It's a nice change. Costigan personifies the healthy scepticism, strong in the Australian community.

He has stuck to his guns.

I can only say one thing to him: "You will not readily be forgiven. But the battlers are with you."

Back to *Power Without Glory*. I have been asked to write *Power Without Glory II*. I'm tempted. I hesitate because I find it difficult to understand what goes on in the minds of todays Mr Bigs.

But beware – I might just have a go. If I made any of the names too close to the bone, I can press a button in a word processor which will select a name far removed. And change it on every bloody page.

Some years ago, I was on the late Sir Frank Packer's hit list of people banned from Channel 9.

I believe this was a result of his objections to certain passages in *Power Without Glory* or to my politics. The list was presumed to be political, but it was a non-descript hotch-potch including some right-wing or non-political people.

The list was secret, of course, but I was more than once supplied with proof that I was on it.

For example, a new producer of the *Don Lane Show*, appointed without being aware of the hit list, Joe Latona booked me to appear – only to have Sir Frank intervene after he heard the ads on 2UE. My daughter, Shirley, took the phone call cancelling my appearance.

I rang Channel 9 and, after a long wait, Lane's writer came on apologetically. He was something of a friend (no names, no Packer drill) and told me that Sir Frank had added a rider to the cancellation: "Hardy needn't worry He'll get plenty of publicity in the *Telegraph* someday. We've got a good obituary written about him."

I eventually appeared on the Lane show and the *Mike Walsh Show*, when Clive Packer was running Channel 9.

Not every card in the pack is a joker.

I should add that I have been reliably informed that one of the many things which led to Clive Packer's departure was the cancellation "over his head" of an appearance by Gough Whitlam and myself about my book, *The Unlucky Australians*.

Recently, an interview with me by Mark Jennings, taped six months ago for the *Mike Willesee Show*, never went to air. It was about the debt-collecting rackets of the finance companies reflected in my novel, *The Obsession of Oscar Oswald*.

A new joker in the Channel 9 pack had told Mike to "lay off the finance companies."

# A Fine Mess

Have you been getting many parking tickets lately? The reason I ask is that I saw in one of the Sydney papers that a large minority of people in Long Bay jail are there for not paying parking fines. I forget the percentage.

But I know that 41 per cent of the population of Bogga Road jail, Brisbane, is made up half of people who owe money to finance companies and the other half by people who haven't paid parking fines.

Neville Wran was kind enough to offer his condolences to people who are in jail. That's all he'll ever do because his government and all the other state governments make much of their revenue from parking fines.

It's a bloody disgrace. Parking facilities in Australian cities are almost non-existent yet they'll put an envelope under your windscreen-wiper fining you $25, or even $80 or more, if you find a parking spot.

If you park in a place where you are not a resident, the situation is worse. You go to the Town Hall in, say, Sydney, and you apply for a resident's sticker and a snotty-nosed bureaucrat tells you that unless you are going to be a permanent resident you can't get one.

Then the fun really starts.

You get a few parking fines every day – then you try to get cunning! You write a sign and put it under your windscreen saying, "Have applied for resident's sticker: please do not give me any more fines or I'll end up in jail."

Far from softening the heart of the Brown Bomber (they must be some kind of monstrosity going around pretending to be human beings), this stratagem only makes that person fine you more often.

Then you try the trick of leaving the first fine under the windscreen-wiper in the misguided belief that the bastard will say, "This car's already been fined about an hour ago; I'll leave it alone for the rest of the day."

But no! He will fine you more often for being cheeky –
and put each fine in the same envelope to save stationery.

On Christmas Eve, they slapped an Enforcement Notice
on a disabled man to jail him for not paying a $25 parking
fine. There are only a dozen parking spots reserved for the
disabled in the city of Sydney.

"Even if you find one, it's usually occupied," the disabled
man said.

"I'd like to know what sort of hard labour I'm going to
do," he added from his wheelchair.

There was an item in a Melbourne newspaper last year
about a man who went to jail for 14 days for not paying
parking fines. (What happens is that after you've failed to
pay the fine, they take you before the court and charge you
extra for costs – with a jail sentence if you don't pay.)

He did his time – he simply didn't have the money to pay
the fine. While he was in jail, he got the sack (most
employers don't like jailbirds.)

He went on the dole, couldn't find another job, then he
got evicted from his house – and his marriage hit trouble.

And all that over bloody parking fines.

As you read this, hundreds of people are in jail for not
paying parking fines.

Yet illegally parking is not a criminal offence; it is a civil
offence; and no jail term can be imposed for a civil offence.

So they are turning people into criminals because they
haven't got the money to pay parking fines.

If I appear to be joking – it is no joking matter. The legal
trick that turns illegal parking into a criminal offence must
be stopped!

It is a similar trick to that used by finance companies and
other sharks to transform the civil offence of debt into a
criminal offence.

People owing money who can't pay it (usually due to
sickness or unemployment) are often dragged before the
courts under the infamous Fraudulent Debtors Act, given
time to pay and if they fail, they go to jail for a few days or a
few months. And they still owe the bloody debt when they
come out.

I wrote a novel on this theme, *The Obsession of Oscar Oswald*, exposing the debt-collection racket and the illegal trans-forming of a civil offence into a criminal offence.

In NSW and Victoria, the legislation is before Parliament to repeal the Fraudulent Debtors Act and revise the Hire Purchase Act, to prevent the worst excesses of the finance sharks.

This legislation came as a result of petitions and agitation by many people and organisations in Melbourne and Sydney, including yours truly.

It is time that the jailing of people for not paying parking fines was brought to a halt. Legislation simply must be brought in.

In the meantime, I've got a couple of suggestions to beat the Brown Bombers.

Sell your motor car.

Or next time you register it, change the address to a street or a number in a street that doesn't exist; this way when the cop comes with the bluey for not paying the fine or fines, he can't bloody find ya. The police don't like jailing people for failing to pay parking fines or debt.

So, if they don't find you first time, they send the summons back to headquarters.

The Collingwood (that is, Carringbush) police in Mel-bourne, and some others, have a very lenient attitude towards victims of the parking fine or debt collecting process. If they happen to find you at home when they bring the summons they ask if it would be convenient for you to serve the time say, at Easter, so you don't lose days off work.

The jails in every city are so full that some victims of parking fines are kept at the local police station, fed well and allowed to use the phone.

Most coppers I've met are crook on the whole system of jailing people for parking fines and debt. Short of using a false address, I suggest that a general strike of motorists be called whenever a motorist is taken to court for not paying a parking fine.

He should go there and say that he can't pay or won't pay!

If enough of us did this, the crooks who run the country would simply have to stop putting people in jail for not paying parking fines because they couldn't build enough bloody jails to accommodate the victims.

If you gather the impression from the above that I'm bloody hostile and that I've received quite a few parking fines lately, you are spot on.

And I've got news for the bastards – I'm not going to pay!

# Hard*yarn*

A mate of mine, "Parking-fine" Patterson, was before the Magistrate's Court over a slight matter of not paying $1000 worth of parking fines.

Old "Parking-fine" was so crook on the system that he always parked his car illegally, as a matter of principle.

He acts very uppity in the court, so the Magistrate says: "I don't like your attitude and I'm going to make an example of you. Unless you pay the fine into the court immediately, plus costs . . ."

"No way known I'm going to pay," says old "Parking-fine" Patterson.

So the Magistrate, snotty-nosed and deaf into the bargain, says: "Alright, then, I'm going to impose a long prison sentence on you. Have you anything to say?"

"No, bugger all!" Patterson replies.

Now, this Magistrate was rather deaf – as I told you. So he says to his associate: "What did he say?"

"Bugger all!" replies the associate.

"That's strange," the Magistrate says, "I could have sworn I saw his lips move."

# The Fine Art of Sledging

During the West Indian cricket tour, I marvelled at the way that quintessentially English game has held the interest of the Australian public for so long.

Cricket, it seems to me, was once used as an instrument of English colonial rule.

The Poms are upset about the black West Indians becoming the best cricketers in the world.

It was bad enough when the Australian team kept beating them in Bradman's day; they resorted to bodyline to put a stop to that.

Australians also seem rather upset by the dominance of the West Indians: Clive Lloyd suggested in one of his newspaper columns that he suspected an element of racism in the reaction here.

I, also found it strange that the Australian players and supporters should complain about the West Indian fast bowlers throwing down the occasional bumper.

After the Lillee-Thomson era, Australia has no cause to complain. Dennis Lillee was the greatest intimidator of batsmen who ever picked up a red ball.

The recent tour also saw the term "sledging" surface in the press. Anyone who knows something of what goes on out there on the field, would know that sledging began with the Australian team in the days of Don Tallon – and later Dennis Lillee and Rodney Marsh got it down to a fine art.

Sledging, for the uninitiated, is a "dirty trick" used by bowlers, wicket-keepers and fielders against batsmen.

For example: let's say – and of course this couldn't possibly happen – that Dennis Lillee is bowling in Perth against a visiting international team and Rodney Marsh is behind the wicket.

First thing – and this also of course couldn't happen – you get the groundsman to doctor the wicket to suit fast bowlers.

Then, when Dennis is running in, Rodney says to, say, Javed Miandad: "Go back to the jungle, you black bastard, you can't play cricket."

Now the old Javed gets a bit upset and it puts him off his game.

. But, somehow, he manages to hang in there and Dennis gets annoyed, blocks him when he's making a run – then kicks him in the arse when he complains (none of which could possibly happen in reality).

That's what they call sledging.

Dennis averaged scores like six for 27 and, of course, he did it on sheer ability.

Strangely enough, I was a keen cricketer in my youth, in sub-district competiton in Melbourne. I won the batting average a couple of times. That was a fluke because in the long one-day games I was often not out as opening batsman in the second innings. That way you build up your average.

I also did quite well as a left-arm bowler; I had a mate at first slip, who used the old "McCool" trick of clicking his thumb and finger when a ball went close to the bat thus giving the umpire the impression that it was a "caught behind" when, in fact, the ball had not touched the bat.

It has been said, perhaps.incorrectly, that many of the extraordinary number of the "caught Tallon, bowled McCool" decisions were arrived at in this manner.

Almost against my will, I retain a deep interest in cricket to this day. Australia, of course, will come back as a great cricket nation if we stop whingeing, give the young blokes a go, and face the fact that the West Indians are just too good, at the moment.

By the way, I should point out that some of my best friends are Poms and cricketers. I have been honoured and much entertained by a long friendship with Fred Trueman, who was, in my opinion, the greatest fast bowler of our time.

We wrote together a book of cricket stories called *You Nearly Had Him That Time.*

My complaint is that in the television series, *Bodyline*, they used two yarns out of the book I wrote with Fred, without payment or acknowledgement.

They had Don Bradman's father being caught by the square-leg umpire; and that was taken from a story I wrote about Sam Loxton, which happened in Bacchus Marsh during the war.

Sam was looking for practice; the square-leg umpire was looking for a drink before the pub shut; Sam hooked one to leg and the square-leg umpire caught it and gave him out. Then both teams went to the pub.

The other yarn pinched by the *Bodyline* mob was the story of Bert Ironmonger's wife ringing the Melbourne Cricket Ground and being told, "hang on Mrs Ironmonger, he's just going in to bat and'll be back in a minute."

Bert only took a bat in with him because he thought it was compulsory.

# *Hardyarn*

Don Tallon had a brother, Bill, didn't he?

And Bill got a few games for Queensland as a medium pace bowler.

Some critics were unkind enough to suggest that he only got in the side because he was the captain's brother.

Bill Tallon had a bad stammer – and had one moment of glory at the Gabba Ground in Brisbane.

This is the story of Bill Tallon's moment of glory, as told by Bill Tallon, as repeated by Wally Grout, as repeated to me by Neil Hawke.

"I'm b-bowling at the G-Gabba and I'm s-swinging it up a b-bit. And I'm b-bowling at a bloke called N-nietschke. He snicks one towards first s-slip – but me b-brother, D-Don, l-leaps across and catches it. One for none!

"A b-bloke called B-Badcock f-faces me n-next. After a w-while, he g-goes for the g-glance and the b-ball flies in the air. F-fine leg went for it, f-first s-slip went for it – but me b-brother, D-Don, ran back and c-caught it. Two for nineteen.

"And who should come in then b-but the g-great D-Don B-Bradman himself. B-But I'm not worried because I'm s-still s-swinging it a bit and g-getting a b-bit of turn off the s-seam.

"And there I am at the G-Gabba b-bowling at D-Don B-Bradman; the g-greatest d-day of me life.

"All of a s-sudden, B-Bradman w-went for a b-big hit. The b-ball w-went so high it d-disappeared into the c-clouds. The l-long on went for it, the l-long off went for it – but me b-brother, D-Don, ran right up the f-field and g-got under it.

"D-Don stood there l-looking into the s-sun, w-waitin' for the b-ball to come d-down – his lips got chafed – b-but he stayed under it and c-caught it.

"Three for two hundred and ninety-six."

# The Funny Side of
# Fiery Fred

A few years ago, I met Keith Miller in the Steyne Hotel, Manly, and said I wanted to earn an honest dollar creating a book of cricket yarns.

Keith, as good a fellow as you'd meet in a day's walk, told me he'd like to collaborate in such a project, but reckoned that the only man in the cricket world for the job was Fiery Freddie Trueman.

In London soon afterwards, I had a job finding the old Fred, but eventually met him for the first time, appropriately enough at Lords cricket ground. Fred was on air as a BBC commentator.

And it was funny; Fred, who turned out to be no lover of Geoffrey Boycott, reacted with less than usual enthusiasm when Boycott reached a record number of centuries. Everybody seemed wildly enthusiastic, except Fred, who merely said in subdued tones – "He's doon it!"

We breasted a bar at lunchtime, and Freddie agreed to work on a humorous cricket book with me. I asked about Boycott and Fred replied: "We'll leave him out of the book; what he's done to cricket isn't funny."

I never did find out the reason for Fred's apparent hostility towards Boycott, but Freddy himself lived up to his reputation as humorous cricket folklorist and outrageous wit.

I've often wondered why men become legends in their own lifetime, when others, of apparently equal ability, do not. I believe it is because they capture the imagination of ordinary people by taking the same attitude as them. This applied to Athol George Mulley as a jockey and to Fred Trueman as a fast bowler.

It was all clear at the first meeting I had with Trueman. A devil-may-care attitude to authority, self-assurance about his own ability without being arrogant, and a humourous turn of phrase which flowed naturally.

Later, I spent a week living at Fred's house in Yorkshire. We would gather at Peter Parfitt's pub with Neil Hawke and other former professional cricketers. They talked shop and I've never laughed so much in my life.

One afternoon, while Peter was busy serving at the bar, Freddie said to me: "Peter was a good left-hand bat, but he had a bad habit of standing on the stumps with his heel when he went for a hook-shot! Ohh-aye! He did it on the Melbourne Cricket Ground one day in a Test against Australia and one of the bails fell off.

"Everyone was watching the ball, see, so nobody noticed, not even the umpire. And there was a photo on the front page of a newspaper the next day, showing Peter putting the bail back on! But no one had noticed it. He went on to make a 100!"

On another occasion, over dinner at Fred's house, he told another story about Peter's bad habit, which is well worth repeating.

There was great rivalry between Lancashire and Yorkshire, and they were playing in Lancashire. One of the umpires thought Peter was a cunning, tricky devil, so he watched him like a hawk, didn't he? Ooh-aye!

A strong wind was blowing. Peter Parfitt went for a hook-shot, tapped the base of one of the stumps with his heel, and a bail fell off! Everyone was watching the ball hurtle to the boundary – except the lousy Lancashire umpire! Peter decided to trick him. "The wind blew the bail off," he said to the umpire, quick as a flash. "It's a very windy day."

The cunning Lancashire umpire replied, "Yes, it's very windy. Thou'd better be careful walking back to the pavilion, or it'll blow yer cap off. I'm giving you out for standing on the wicket!"

Fred Trueman reckoned that the rivalry between Yorkshire and Lancashire in those days was so great that a certain Lancashire captain invented a prayer to be used in every match against Yorkshire.

He'd arrive at the ground before everyone else, kneel down in the shower and say The Lancashire Lord's Prayer:

"Dear Lord – Thou'd be the best judge of a cricket match in all the world. And today, if Yorkshire is the best team, they will win; if Lancashire is the best team, we will win; if the teams are equal, the game will be drawn; if it rains cats and dogs, the game will be abandoned. But if Thou will keep tha' bloody nose out of it, Lancashire will win by an innings! Amen!"

Fred was often in trouble with the Marylebone Cricket Club during his long career. He got into a lot of trouble during one tour of India and the MCC often fined him large sums.

Fred denies the apocryphal story which had him saying to a Maharajah at a dinner: "Pass the sugar, Gunga Din," but he admits he stepped out of line quite a few times.

He shrugged off the heavy fines and suspensions with typical wit: "They fined me so often that when I got back to England, I owed the Marylebone Cricket Club money and me wife wanted to know where I'd been all winter!"

Using a tape recorder in the pub over dinner, and at Fred's famous stand-up comic performances, I got down about 16 of Fred's yarns, wrote the same number myself about Australian cricket, and we made up a few stories together.

One night late, I asked Fred if he'd ever struck what we call in Australia a "fluker". Ooh-aye! Fred had struck a few all right, hadn't he! So we bounced one-liners about fluking lucky batsmen between our pipes and beer glasses. After an hour, we had a story called *The Fluker*.

It's too long to relate here (you'll have to buy the bloody book to get the details), but some idea of it's flavour can be gleaned from Fred's remark that he struck a Lancashire fluker who had the "play and miss" shot down to a fine art.

My meetings with Fred Trueman were a sheer delight, and we wrote a book to prove that cricket, like grand opera, is funniest at its most serious moments.

# *Hardyarn*

My favourite yarn of Fred Trueman's concerns none other than Douglas Jardine, of bodyline infamy, him-sodding-self.

Yorkshire were playing Cambridge. There had been some rain and the wicket was a Sticky Dog.

A certain Yorkshire bowler worked as a miner during the winter, and hated all amateur cricketers, – the Fancy Caps, as he called them

Yorkshire won the toss and sent Cambridge in to bat. The conditions suited the bowler (we'll say it was Mick Cowan), and he got two Cambridge wickets very quickly and cheaply. Cambridge were two for 27, and Mick had two for 11.

And who should Mick Cowan see coming in to bat, but the future amateur captain of England himself – Douglas Snobbynose Jardine!

Mick wants his wicket bad!

Douglas Jardine walks to the wicket in all his glory, wearing an expensive Viyella shirt, a Fancy Cap, silk batting gloves and handmade boots. Mick reckoned he had 500 quid's worth of clothes on!

One of the fieldsmen asked Mick: "Where's he going, then?"

"I don't know," Mick Cowan replied, "but he smells nice!"

Douglas Jardine went to a lot of trouble taking block, had a good look around to see if any of the Yorkshire tykes had moved in the meantime, then checked his bat with the umpire again.

"Let's get on wi' t'game, then," Mick demanded.

And when Jardine was ready, he bowled a leg break that sent the off-stump tumbling over.

Jardine, the future amateur captain of England, looked at the wicket in disbelief. He'd been bowled first ball by a common miner, who'd never even played for England! But, being a gentleman, he walked towards the pavilion with his bat under his arm, taking off one of his gloves.

As he walked past Mick Cowan he said condescendingly: "Well bowled, Cowan! That was a good ball!"

And Mick Cowan replied: "Aye, but it were wasted on thee!"

# Capital Offensives

Recently, the wife of some Birthday Knight declared in the Sydney Press that Melbourne restaurants were generally better than Sydney restaurants.

Them's fightin' words, Lady!

It's not the right thing to praise Melbourne restaurants in Sydney; it's as bad as praising Sydney beer in Melbourne.

I thought the Melbourne-Sydney argument was settled years ago but still the odd battle is fought.

Nowhere else in the world can people be found doing the lolly over the real and imagined virtues of the two cities. In America, they argue about Los Angeles and New York; in Russia they argue about Moscow and Leningrad; but not with the snide, cunning, sarcastic wit of a citizen of Melbourne making satirical references to Sydney or vice versa.

They don't have this problem in France: no Frenchman would dare to even suggest that any other city in France, or anywhere in the bloody world, would remotely compare to gay Paree; whether for wine, women, song, or even punting; all Frenchmen agree that Paris is the centre of the world. I would take issue with the French about punting: facilities for gambling on horses are better in Australia than in Paris or anywhere else.

Where did the Melbourne-Sydney argument begin?

In Melbourne and Sydney! Where the hell else?

It really got warmed up at the turn of the century, when the Australian states decided to federate and the Sydney mob declared that, naturally, Sydney should be the capital of the new nation. Of course, the Melbourne mob had different ideas. And a great, long winded argument began, which looked like ending in civil war when the Federal Parliament made its headquarters in Melbourne.

And this is where Australian ingenuity came to the

rescue: some cunning bastard worked out that war could be avoided if they set up a new capital city on New South Wales soil and pretended to the Melbourne mob that it was not really in NSW but was a separate capital territory called Canberra.

Of course, this did not stop the Melbournians and the Sydneyites having the occasional argument, slanging match or grass fight over such fundamental issues as beer, race horses and football.

Now, I've always believed that I should remain neutral in this uncivil war. With that laudable aim in view, I've spent exactly half my life in Victoria and half in NSW (that's if you don't count four years in France.)

In 1952, Rosslyn and I, dyed-in-the-wool Victorians from way back, were having a rather rough time in Melbourne and decided to leave Victoria for the good of our health. We took the train to Sydney, friends drove us to Palm Beach – and the golden chain of surf and sand impelled us to do a moonlight flit and live in Manly.

I found Sydney little different from Melbourne – except I couldn't stomach Sydney beer.

This problem I solved by drinking at the single hotel in Sydney that served Richmond beer (a great brew which dried up when taken over by Carlton and United Breweries, the mob who make Fosters).

Then Scoop Wilson, the poet laureate of the Fisho's Club in Manly, advised me to try Reschs. "It's a good brew, mate, and you're gonna get kicked to death if you keep knocking Sydney beer around this town."

So I became a fervent convert (and unless I get a crate of Reschs beer delivered to *People* within a week, I'll switch to Tooheys New!)

If I were forced into a dangerous corner and had to sum up, I'd say that Sydney and Melbourne are different – but equal. For me, the big difference is that a horse called Carringbush and the Carringbush Library exist in Melbourne. But I wrote *Power Without Glory* there and called the suburb of Collingwood Carringbush. Perhaps you could call that an accident of history. However, *Power Without Glory* is on TV in Sydney as I write – and not in Melbourne.

Anyway, the Australian battler is the same everywhere: ironic, sceptical – and a loyal friend.

# *Hardy*arn

I actually settled the Melbourne-Sydney argument years ago on neutral territory.

There was a pub on the Victorian and NSW border which served Melbourne and Sydney beer to an equal mix of citizens from both states.

I drank there with two blokes called Melbourne Mick and Sydney Sam. They were the best of mates, fought in some war together, worked together, drank together but would argue in an empty house when it came to Melbourne and Sydney.

They might start by making sly little jokes about the harbour bridge being an oversized coathanger, or the Yarra the only river in the world that flows upside down. Melbourne Mick would say: "The only city in the world where they have a public holiday for a horse race."

And Sydney Sam would come back: "But more Sydney than Melbourne jockeys have ridden the Cup winner in the past 10 years."

So they'd switch to jockeys. Sydney Sam would talk about Athol Mulley riding more winners every season than any Melbourne jockey. And Melbourne Mick would quote how Scobie Breasley won the English jockey's premiership two years in a row.

So they'd switch to horses and go at it hammer and tongs. Melbourne Mick would end up quoting Phar Lap's record; and Sydney Sam would refer to Tulloch's stake winnings.

Well, I used to drink with them, see, and I was a neutral in the Melbourne-Sydney war. So I'd say "Both Phar Lap and Tulloch are New Zealand-bred horses."

They came to blows more than once about football. Melbourne Mick would say: "Australian Rules draws bigger crowds in Melbourne than Rugby in Sydney."

"What?" Sydney Sam would say, "that's not football, mate, it's aerial ping-pong."

That aerial ping-pong crack was always good for a fight in the pub yard. After the fight, Melbourne Mick would start the argument again. "In Rugby they throw the ball all the time. A good Australian Rules player would kick a goal on a Rugby ground from the other end."

Then I would intervene, see. "Hang on a minute, don't either of you realise that the only true game of football is soccer? They use the feet only, real football."

I thought that would have settled it, but in the next six weeks they had six fights over the climate in Melbourne and Sydney and six over the Yarra and the Harbour Bridge.

After that, I worked overtime to convince them that Melbourne and Sydney were different but equal, and they had no more fights in the pub about football, the Yarra and the Bridge, horses and jockeys, climate or migration.

Then they started to fight over population and I broke it up by explaining that, while Sydney had a bigger population, Melbourne was growing faster.

But even a Philadelphia lawyer or a Yankee diplomat couldn't have stopped them having a fight every pay night – about beer.

Melbourne Mick drank Melbourne Beer and Sydney Sam drank Sydney beer, needless to say. And they'd needle each other.

"Melbourne beer has a higher alcoholic content," Mick would say. "That's why there's more alcoholics in Melbourne than Sydney," Sam would reply.

"Sydney beer is thick and frothy like a milk shake," Melbourne Mick would argue. "Everybody knows Melbourne beer is the best. Some say it's because the water is more suitable."

This would give Sam an opening. "I always knew Melbourne beer was watered." That was good for another fight. I tried everything to stop them. Even got the barman to serve Mick Sydney beer and Sam Melbourne beer.

They knew the difference. They each took one sip, spat it out and said: "What, are you trying to poison me?" They had so many fights I was worried they would end up punchy.

So one night, I says to them: "Listen, mates, these arguments and fights over Melbourne and Sydney beer have got to stop. Tell you what I'll do. I'll send a sample of the best Melbourne and Sydney beer to the CSIRO for analysis. Will you abide by their decision?"

Mick and Sam were both of a scientific turn of mind so they agreed to abide by any decision made by the CSIRO.

I scraped the labels off a bottle of Sydney and Melbourne beer, marked them A and B and sent them off with a letter.

Then Melbourne Mick and Sydney Sam began to fight over the likely result of the test.

Eager for an answer I sent a reply-paid telegram to the CSIRO.

And back came the answer: "Thorough tests made stop Regret inform you both horses have colic."

# Punting in Paris

Between 1976 and 1980 I spent most of my time in France, mainly in a southern village, St Paul de Vence.

The only way you can get to know a foreign people is to live in their country, and the only way you can get to know your own country is to live outside it for a while.

During my first few months in St Paul, I didn't have a bet.

I suffered severe withdrawal symptoms, but had plenty of time on my hands and in 26 days wrote a novel set in Melbourne called *Who Shot George Kirkland*.

Then one morning I went to a little cafe inside the walls of the 12th century village to find it packed with punters studying form guides of all sizes and all different colours, and making bets with a woman who sat behind a table in the corner.

I was delighted to find that horse-playing flourished but said to meself: "This is a restaurant; must be an illegal SP – and it's bloody Sunday!"

Well, it was a Sunday morning all right and, when I glanced over a shoulder at a form guide, I discovered that they were racing at Longchamps.

As I was soon to find out, the horses race in France seven days a week and 365 days in the year – including Good Friday and Christmas Day.

And France is the only country on earth where they publish a daily newspaper devoted to horse racing.

I discussed this astonishing and welcome fact with actor Yves Montand who claimed that the French spent more money on gambling than any other people. "My go is stud poker," he said. "But if you want to play the horses you came to the right country."

Outside the little cafe was a sign PMU (short for Pari Mutuel), which is the French equivalent of the TAB signs seen all over Australia.

I was to learn that all PMUs in France were franchised to cafes and bars and restaurants (with the exception of a few mammoth tote shops in Paris).

Imagine the old Hardy occupying a table in a restaurant, studying the form with a glass of beer or wine at his elbow and having a lunch of rich French sausages and salad. A bit of a change from the dingy TAB shops in Melbourne and Sydney where there was nothing to eat or drink, not even a chair or a toilet.

I gather that the French constitution forbids the government to profit from gambling, so the cunning Frogs sublet the tote betting to restauranteurs and publicans – not forgetting, of course, to rake in the same percentage as the government takes in Australia.

As well as daily race meetings, mainly gallops, there are, in season, trotters (no pacers) and jumping events. And the hurdles at (say) Longchamps are so high that the average Australian jumper would have to stop, go back and have another run at them.

The most remarkable feature of gambling on horses in France is the famous Tierce, conducted in every off-course PMU across the country on the main race every Thursday and Sunday.

The Tierce has to be experienced to be believed. The coverage of form for those two races every week is more extensive than that given in the Australian press to the Melbourne Cup.

And the pool at the PMU runs into millions of francs. With the Tierce, you have to pick the first three horses in "ordre" or "ordre different". Picking the first three horses in order is the same as the Australian Trifecta; picking them in different order is a Trio. So the Tierce is both a Trifecta and a Trio.

You can take a minimum of three horses or a maximum of nine in combination and, of course, the dividends vary according to the price of the horses.

Dividends of more than 1000 francs were common, of more than 10,000 francs not uncommon, of more than 100,000 francs not unknown.

France would be an Australian racing punter's paradise.

The daily racing paper I refer to (it's called Paris Turf but pronounced Pari Tur) publishes a monthly called the Turfists Memoir which shows up to date ratings for every horse registered in France; and Paris Turf itself rates each horse for every meeting and gives the weight it should carry according to their ratings beside the weight it is to carry.

There is a lotto and, of course, casinos in France but the most popular form of gambling is the bi-weekly Tierce – even for people who have never been on the race course in their lives.

On one occasion Nana Mouskouri, herself a non gambler (I guess because her father was such a reckless roulette player) once expressed to me astonishment that the news on French television channels on Thursday and Sunday nights always began with the Tierce race: the last two furlongs and the dividends, win and place, Trifecta and Trio.

I had to explain to her patiently that this was perfectly understandable because most viewers would switch to another channel if the racing news didn't come on first.

I spent the winter of 1979 in Paris writing a film script for an Australian-French co-production called *The Last Big Bet*. One of the central characters was a Frenchman living in Melbourne and some of the scenes were set in Paris. (Needless to say, the film was never made.) A pity that! It explained how the professionals rated horses!

In Paris, I really got to know the French racing scene and my yarns about Australian horse racing were well received. Australian jockeys are held in high esteem: Athold Mulley, the late Nifty Neville Selwood, George and Gary Moore (Gary rides with great success in Paris to this day) and Jimmy Johnstone (the French punters call him Jimmy the Crocodile because of the way he seemed to lay flat over a horse's neck).

In Melbourne and Sydney, I've heard many violent demonstrations over jockeys or form reversals – but the French punters would play us on a break.

One day at Longchamps, the stewards instituted a protest in a race where there was some jostling in the straight.

The favourite had won, ridden by Lester Piggott, not usually the most popular jockey in the world with French horse players. (I once sent him a press cutting from *Paris Turf* which clearly revealed the crowd booing just before he passed the winning post.)

After 20 minutes, the stewards changed the placings and the winning favourite was left out. Lester Piggott or no Lester Piggott, the crowd went berserk. Furious punters lined the fence of the mounting yard hurling unprintable insults at the Commissaire de la Course (Chief Steward).

Apparently of the opinion that he could not hear them from his office on the second floor of the stand (which runs the full length of the straight with bars, restaurants and automatic totes where you buy your tote tickets from a slot machine), a few punters climbed the rail and stood on the track right in front of the Chief Steward's office. They were soon joined by hundreds more and, in spite of appeals from officials over the sound system, refused to budge to allow the next race to be run.

In desperation, the Commissaire de la Course announced that the steward's "head-on" shots of the last furlong of the race would be shown on the internal television.

The trick worked; the punters on the track climbed back over the fence to look at the stewards' pictures.

Soon, most were convinced that the stewards' decision was correct.

But more than an hour had passed and darkness began to fall before the last race – which had to be abandoned.

I said earlier that facilities for gambling on horses are better in Australia than in France. And that's true, in some respects: mainly because the PMU closes at one o'clock each afternoon, so that you virtually have to place all your bets before the first race and can't get paid until the next morning. Enough said? Perhaps this has changed for the better since 1980. I do hope so because an irate City Extra listener in Sydney rang in to say that I should go back to France.

# *Hardyarn*

Horror of horrors! While I was in Paris, the PMU went on strike for higher wages!

Now, one of the pleasing differences between Australia

and France is that the French are generally more tolerant about strikes.

A fairly typical view was expressed to me by a taxi driver during a long, drawn-out strike of the cleaners in the Metro (underground railway); in spite of the fact that you couldn't get into the Metro without walking through rubbish up to your knees, he said: "I look at it this way: they must have a good reason for such a long strike and if they get a rise others might benefit."

In fact, any group of workers could go on strike in France and be assured of fairly wide support – except the employees of the PMU.

The PMU strike started on a Sunday.

Unaware of this fateful event I sauntered down the Rue de la Boucherie to consult my fellow Turfist, the owner of a Vietnamese restaurant on the corner; Ho informed me, more in sorrow than in anger, that the PMU workers were on strike. He told me that one of the big betting shops was open but you couldn't get near it even by taxi.

Certain that I had the Tierce solved, I grabbed a cab. When told where I was going, the taxi driver said that it was coming to something when the working man couldn't have a bet on the PMU because of a *merde greve*.

Anyway, he got me to within a few blocks of the PMU building: he could go no further because of the crowd. So I walked the rest of the way pushing my way past disgruntled punters until I reached the entrance of the huge building, which had tote windows along each side. Instead of queues at each window, clusters of people jostled each other in a huge half circle. I joined one of these clusters and only gave up when a woman who had just laid her bets fainted and her limp body was passed over the head of the crowd into the arms of a couple of gendarmes.

# An Idiot's Delight

There is a theory in the television business that only about 1000 people in the whole of Australia regularly get interviewed on television.

They are recycled again and again simply because they can answer instead of drying up like most people when confronted with a camera.

During the first years of Australian television, which began in 1956, I was never interviewed – I was on Frank Packer's hit list, and the other channels didn't much fancy the idea of putting that bloody commo who wrote *Power Without Glory* on the idiot box.

However, Dr Clement Semmler, then program manager of the ABC, put my *Billy Borker Yarns* on television, and Bill Munro, the producer, cast me in the program *Would You Believe?* with Jackie Weaver et al.

I soon proved myself to be the biggest and most amusing liar in the southern hemisphere, which led everyone, except me old mate Sir Frank, to want to shove me on television as an interviewee.

It is quite easy when you get the knack – like being in the witness box in court, answer up quickly as if you're telling the truth.

I think my first appearance on television was with Bill Peach on the very first program of *This Day Tonight*.

After the success of *Would You Believe?* I found myself in danger of becoming the token Lefty of Australian television. So I says to meself about 15 years ago: "I'll have to kick this habit."

But what does a reformed television interviewee do when he wants to get some free publicity for new book? He lets his publisher organise a nationwide tour of television interviews, doesn't he? Except on Channel 9, of course.

Then, bugger me if I don't win a Logie (in 1970 I think it

was) which meant a live appearance on Channel 9, a free air ticket to Melbourne and a suite in the Southern Cross Hotel.

I was pissed as a newt by the time Bert Newton announced that I had won a Logie for a TV script, *The Daybreak Killer*.

I didn't forget to tell Sir Frank that I was live on Channel 9 and to remind him that he should take his green pill and his white pill before going to sleep.

Next day, back in Sydney, I invited a few friends to watch the re-run of the Logie awards. The unedifying picture of a drunken author accepting a Logie with such lack of gratitude and good grace had been deleted!

Since then, I have done hundreds of television interviews in Australia and beyond, giving it up from time to time (it's as easy as giving up smoking – you can do it many times).

My most startling and strange interview on the idiot box was the one I did with Michael Parkinson a few years ago.

So there I am, in the green room at the ABC's Gore Hill studios, waiting to go on after Paul Hogan who is a hard bloody act to follow.

Michael Parkinson introduced me in a friendly manner – but soon me and Parkie were locked in heated political argument with Paul Hogan playing a kind of Aussie chorus of brilliant ad-libbed one-liners, sometimes sending up Parkinson and sometimes, meself.

At one stage, Parkinson got upset and told the studio audience and viewers that, far from being a right-winger, he was a miner's son and had never voted Tory in his life.

Hoges quipped: "Don't worry too much about Frank – he's an institution and if the communists came to power in Australia, he'd join the Liberal Party."

At the end of the game, the scores were Hogan 10, Hardy 1 and Parkinson nil.

I was really forced to kick the habit when, in London, I called Prince Phillip "Phil, the Greek" on Thames television; then returning to Australia five years ago, never again to leave, I said the fatal word "f . . .!" on the ABC.

After that, I didn't get any requests to go on television for a long, long time.

But Australian television channels, even including Channel 9 occasionally (since the untimely death of Sir Frank) can't resist a man with a big mouth, a sense of humour and controversial opinions.

So I remained hooked: *60 Minutes, The Mike Walsh Show, Good Morning Australia*, you name it, and I've been on it.

And now with *Who Was Harry Larsen?* likely to have a long journey, you'll be seeing my ugly skull and hearing my raspy voice, acting like an idiot on the idiot box until the year 2000.

God help you all, dear citizens of Australia.

## *Hardyarn*

Several years ago in London, an interviewer asked me what would happen to my communistic views, seeing that I had become rich through the *Power Without Glory* television series? The poor fellow didn't seem to know I had received less than $1000 an episode for the series.

My reply: "I would become more revolutionary than ever, because a poor man can't really afford to be a communist."

This highly amused Yves Montand, who lived with Signoret in the same block of flats as I did for a while in St Paul de Vence, France.

Yves, who had suffered for years the strange accusation that he had no right to be communistic when he had become very rich from his movies, capped my quip with the best answer I have ever heard to a loaded TV question.

Montand drove from St Paul to Monaco in a Rolls-Royce to be interviewed by a woman personality with a Sunday afternoon show.

After leading Yves up the garden path of discussing his left-wing views in detail, the lady asked cunningly: "Don't you think it strange that a communist should arrive at a television station in a new Rolls-Royce?"

Quick as a flash, Yves replied: "Better a communist in a Rolls-Royce than a Fascist in a tank!"

# Death to Inheritance!

My father always said that every man and woman in Australia should have the right to introduce one law into the statute books – in the public interest.

Many years ago, we sometimes played a game of picking the law we would like to establish.

My father always chose a law which would make inheritance illegal. "Cancel the bloody law of inheritance and most of the problems of the world would be solved," he used to say.

And, in this day and age, looking at some of the characters who have inherited great wealth, I'm inclined to think that Old Tom had something (although admittedly, at the time, we thought he must have been crazy).

I remember only vaguely the variations he used to play on his theme but, applying it to our time, the mind boggles at the radical changes which would take place in our society.

Think of all the trouble that would be saved about assets tests. Who would give a stuff about having their assets tested if, as well as not being able to take their assets with them, they couldn't leave them to their relations.

*The Gillies Report* had a wonderful skit of an old man pottering about the garden and saying: "Another thing, my kids are showing too much interest in my assets test." He seemed to live in funny fear that they would knock him off so as to get their hands on his assets.

I've never been involved in the inheritance of money – except when Don Rountree left me 500 pounds in his will, in the certain belief that he would live longer than I would.

I put the money on Nebo Road in its second Newmarket and it was beaten by half a head by Manihi, ridden by Harry White. Athol George Mulley rode Nebo Road, of course.

The horses bumped near the post and Mulley thought it was his fault. When viewing a film of the finish on the next

Monday, one of the stewards commented: "Manihi bored out – if Mulley had protested, he would have got the race."

Which only goes to show that my father was right when he said no good ever came of inheriting money.

Henry Lawson's will concluded with the immortal words: "There is nothing wrong with me – except financial troubles."

Another famous will was made by Joe Hill, the American anarchist, who was immortalised in the song *I Dreamed I Saw Joe Hill Last Night*. It was written, I think, by Woody Guthrie.

Joe Hill's will took the form of a quatrain:
"My will is easy to decide
For there is nothing to divide
My friends don't need to fuss or moan
Moss does not cling to a rolling stone."

The American Constitution (or was it the Declaration of Independence) contains the beautiful phrase: All men are born equal.

And, if you're lame-brained, you will believe that all Americans (and Australians) are born equal.

My father would have said that some are born more equal than others. When you come to think of it, and look at the matter fairly just for once in your life, the cancellation of the law of inheritance would do one hell of a lot of good.

Every man, woman and child comes into the world with nothing – and should go out with nothing. The only way to ensure this is to make it a crime to leave money or property to anybody.

I knew an old bloke in Bacchus Marsh years ago who won the lottery. He and his wife spent the lot in six years. The bloke's name was Sandy Mitchell, who explained that he was glad he'd spent it because if he'd left it to his kids, they might have turned out to be snobs or scabs.

I can hear the people reading *People* ask: "What would become of the money and property if it couldn't be inherited?"

Being as wise or as foolish as Socrates himself, I will answer the question with another question:

Why are publishers falling over themselves at the moment publishing dozens of books by Henry Lawson?

I'll answer my own question (which I admit is a bad habit): they are rushing to publish Lawson because his works are now out of copyright – and it costs them nothing in royalties.

They call this the public domain. After the passage of a certain time, an author's works (in other words his assets) pass into the public domain.

I am beginning to think that any of us who thought my father was a mug were fools.

## *Hardyarn*

When my father used to play the game of each putting forward a law they wanted instituted, an old mate named Artie MacIntosh used to always say: "Fences should be made illegal!"

Now Artie took this view because he earned his living, at the time, as a posthole digger and fencer.

But just think of the problems that would be solved if there were no fences, not even frontier fences!

# Truthful Jones on Raffles

There I am in the Carringbush Hotel, Collingwood, drinking with the flies.

And I'm there for a good reason: some people bought a run-down pub near the railway line – and changed its name to the Carringbush Hotel.

What did they pay me who invented the word Carringbush in *Power Without Glory*? One free counter lunch! That's what!

So I hang about the pub, occasionally dropping hints that some sort of honorarium should be paid for the use of the name. But my hints fall on stony ground – like the seed in the Bible.

I'm just about to get maudlin about the injustice of the world. Well, can you blame me? There's a Carringbush library, a Carringbush racehorse, a Carringbush architects' office, and the odd fish shop or boutique – all called bloody Carringbush.

Then, I tell myself, it's a great honour, really, to have invented a name and have it pass into the language of my home city, when who should walk in but Truthful Jones himself.

"What are you doing here?" he asks.

"I might ask you the same question. Last time we met, you were up at Billinudgel . . ."

After admitting the fact, Truthful says he's come to Melbourne to set up a raffle business, to suss out suitable pubs.

"I thought raffles had gone out of fashion," says I.

"Not in Marvellous Melbourne, they haven't," Truthful says. "In fact, I ran the only fair dinkum raffle in Melbourne. Did I ever tell you about it?"

"No, I don't think you did. Have a drink and bash me ear."

"It happened during the '30s Depression years. Things

was crook with me at the time and I was no Robinson Crusoe, I can tell you. Funny thing about a depression. The silvertails always say the unemployed don't want to work, then comes a war and there's no more unemployed. Now where do them unemployed get to? Killed in the war, I s'pose."

"You could be right at that – but get on with your story."

"You're a bit niggly today," comments Truthful Jones slyly. "Could it be that you failed to copyright the name Carringbush and never got a brass razoo for all these places called after it?"

He downed his beer without removing the glass from his lips and waxed philosophical: "Buying raffle tickets is a bad habit to get into, like paying your income tax and backing racehorses – once you start, you can't stop. I've run a few raffles in my time, and I know what I'm talking about."

"Oh, I don't know. A lot of honest raffles are run, I reckon."

"Well, every man's entitled to his own opinion – but opinions are funny things – a man who gets wrong opinions either ends up in jail or in Parliament."

"You'd better tell me about that raffle . . . what was it again?"

"The only fair dinkum raffle ever run in Melbourne. I ran it myself, so I ought to know . . . There was a bloke next door to me who kept chooks. Out at Preston it was.

"I used to keep looking over the fence at them fowls, clucking and pecking away, and I used to say to meself: 'Them chooks are eating their heads off in there while human beings are starving. It isn't right. Them chooks ought to be raffled.'

"So one night, I dives over the fence and grabs two big black chooks. Orphingtons they were. You wouldn't credit the noise a chook can make when it knows it's going to be raffled – fit to wake their owner up. At last, I get hold of 'em and put 'em in a bag under the bed."

"And what has stealing two chooks got to do with a fair dinkum raffle?"

"Coming to that – not a bad drop of beer this – well, next

day was Saturday and I went down to the pub. And I've got these two chooks in a spud bag with their heads stickin' out of two holes.

"Threepence a ticket – threepence was a lot of dough in those days. Well, I sold a book of tickets, and just to show it was fair dinkum, I asked the publican to draw it."

"But how could the raffle be fair dinkum? Have another drink."

"Well, a fella named Smith won the chooks. A little fella with sandy hair and a white-handled pocket knife. So I gave him the two chooks, bag and all. Think he'd won the lottery."

"But what about your next door neighbour? You stole his chooks."

"Coming to that. I had a guilty conscience about stealing them chooks, so I follows this fella Smith home. It's getting dark. He goes in and tells his missus about the chooks, then puts 'em out in the wood-shed. I'm hanging round the front gate and watching and listening in the night. When the lights in the house go out, I snuck into Smith's wood-shed and pinched the two chooks."

"And gave them back to the original owner?"

"That's for sure. The only fair dinkum raffle . . ."

"Just a minute. That fella Smith who won the raffle. He paid for his ticket – threepence," I argues.

"Well, I thought of that. So after I returned the chooks to their owner, I went back to Smith's place and pushed a thrupenny bit under his front door . . ."

"You win. I must admit you tell a good story."

"That reminds me, did I ever tell you about the crookest raffle ever run in Australia?"

"I've to to go now. You can tell me tomorrow."

"Won't be here tomorrow. I'll be raffling a couple of turkeys in a pub out at Preston."

# *Hardyarn*

A famous raffle king in Footscray known as Raffles Rogers used to raffle meat in a certain pub. Some of his clients suspected he got it from Angliss' meatworks. He refused to comment.

Eventually, Sir William Angliss, who didn't believe any employee had the right to be a thief, had a policeman placed at the gate of his abattoirs.

Even our famous Raffles Rogers had difficulty getting past. One day he said to a copper who demanded he open his Gladstone bag: "I've got a cat in there – it'll escape."

The copper insisted and sure enough a black cat leapt out and dashed back through the gate.

"You stupid bastard!" the raffle king said, coming back after retrieving the cat. "It took me half an hour to find it."

The policeman didn't search the bag again; and next time it was full of meat.

# Crime: Organised or Inherited?

The press recently carried extracts from a book about the late and unlamented Sir Robert Askin.

The book documented what every well-informed person in Sydney knew in Askin's lifetime – that he was a crook and stood at the centre of a network of corruption which involved policemen, politicians, crime big-shots and businessmen.

Sir Robert left more than $3 million. Did he save up from his pay as Premier or win it at the races or in poker schools?

The book quoted a chief of police as saying, during the Askin era, that there was no such thing as organised crime.

An earlier Police Commissioner had said that Thommo's Two Up School did not exist. A few days after the report of this statement, I grabbed a random taxi and said: "Thommo's please." The driver took me straight there.

But the top cop who said there was no such thing as organised crime might have uttered an unintended truth.

Now, dear people who read *People*, I want you to look at this matter fairly and without blinkers just for once.

To speak of organised crime is to conjure up a vision of sinister criminals, the Mr Bigs who are rarely named and never arrested, working outside "respectable society" by doing all sorts of naughty things like running SP joints and brothels or selling drugs that are illegal (as distinct from the cigarette companies whose drugs are legal).

The notorious Mr Asia was supposed to be a Mr Big but he turned out to be a mad dog who had to keep killing people whom he feared would turn him in.

He'd have been safe in NSW but he made the mistake of doing one of his murders in England and the Pommie cops grabbed him. In jail, he suffered the same fate as his own victims – he was murdered to prevent him from talking.

Intelligent, sceptical, Australian battlers, like meself, know that crime is not organised – it is institutionalised.

Nifty Neville Wran is probably the unluckiest man in Australia. Nifty's probably had his share of good luck but his bad luck was that he inherited, I would say unwillingly, the sinister problem of institutionalised crime which had begun in the Joe Cahill Labor era and was enlarged and refined by Sir Robert Askin himself.

In Askin's days, I made my only visit to the dining room of the NSW Parliament and who, you may ask, was sitting at the next table? No less a person than lovable Lennie McPherson himself. I gathered he was a regular visitor as part of the quite blatant connection between the so-called criminal world and the "respectable" world of politics and "legitimate" business.

In America, the Mafia and big business are so overlapped that no one knows anymore which business is Mafia controlled or is an "honest" national or multinational corporation.

The point is, there is no longer any sharp dividing line between organised crime and big business, with sections of the judiciary and the police inevitably involved.

Several members of the Reagan administration have been charged with criminal offences in recent years.

And, for instance, a certain flogger of plastic money is now under Mafia control. Nothing has changed with this plastic card company except the owners.

The other side of this sinister coin is the connection of "respectable big business" with the criminal world and its use of people with violent criminal records to, at the end of the line, enforce payment of the money owing to them.

The biggest finance companies in Australia are owned by banks, who send their least well-heeled borrowers down the road where they pay astronomical interest rates on hire purchase contracts, etc.

Now, these battling customers are the most likely to be unable to pay. This is compensated for by the fact that a flat rate of 15.5 per cent interest, which turns into 230 per cent on a four-year contract, is charged.

The finance companies hand their bad debts over to commercial agents or mercantile companies, who employ the very toughest men, some with criminal records, to intimidate the victims, break into their houses to repossess goods or grab their cars on which the payments are behind.

Various Royal Commissions have named well-known business personalities as being connected with organised crime. The point is, however, that big business has traditionally been involved with criminal activities of a "legal" kind. Now big crime and big business are merging.

In NSW, the Chief Magistrate is in jail, two judges are before the courts (at least one was as unlucky as Nifty because *The Age* tapes and *The National Times* were very selective: revealing criminal activity connected with the Labor Party, not the Liberal Party).

Yet the very fabric of the combination of big business and big crime was perfected under the Askin Liberal Government.

In the abovementioned Royal Commissions, a couple of Knights of the Realm were named (but not nabbed).

Robert Askin was a Knight of the Realm. He appointed himself and he was a criminal. And he sold knighthoods for a fee as high as $60,000. So the word Sir before a person's name does not necessarily mean that he is respectable. And the going price for seats in the Upper House was, at that time, $12,000 for both Liberal and Labor members.

Nifty Neville is showing signs that he is prepared to do something about the problem he inherited from Askin. I do hope he will follow through and knock off not only bent cops, magistrates and actual criminals but some of the respectable businessmen, including Knights of the Realm.

# *Hardyarn*

Our yarn this week is a fairytale.

Once upon a time, and it's no good askin' me when, there was a big gambling game known as a poker school. The stakes were high so only the richest in the land attended and they included a tycoon and the leader of the state.

The tycoon was a skilful player and the leader was, in the quaint language of the day, a mug. Soon the leader of the

State owed the tycoon a lot of money. And the tycoon spoke to him, saying: "I'll settle for a knighthood."

And so it came to pass, that a tough tycoon, a pharisee and a profiteer, became a Knight of the Realm.

And the people rejoiced because both the leader of the State and the tycoon were knighted by Her Majesty, the Queen of all the queer doings. The people knew that all was well in the best of all worlds.

And everybody lived happily ever after.

# Footie Fever in Chinkapook

I'm an Aussie Rules man myself. There I was at the Fitzroy - St Kilda match early in the season thinking: What's happened to the Lions? At half-time, they looked like losing to St Kilda.

Before I go any further I must let you in on one of the dark secrets of my life – I don't barrack for Carringbush (for that read Collingwood).

I became a Fitzroy supporter when I was four, for reasons I can't remember. I tried to switch to Collingwood in 1951, after I'd immortalised it in *Power Without Glory*, but found that football is like religion: you can't change from the church you're brought up in.

And who should interrupt my thoughts that day at the football? You've guessed it! Truthful Jones himself!

Truthful sat down beside me, complete with Esky, a woollen cap, the *Football Record* and all the other paraphernalia appropriate to the occasion.

"Goodday," said Truthful.

"What are you doin' here?" I replied. "Thought you were a Rugby man."

"I'm a supporter of all codes – Aussie Rules, Soccer, League and Union. Can't wear that Yankee Gridiron they bung on Channel Nine . . . no skill in it – the brainless against the muscle-bound, if you ask me."

Truthful gave me a sly look, and asked: "What are *you* doin' here? Thought you were a Collingwood barracker."

After I'd explained it was a question of religion, Truthful bought me a drink for the first time in his life! He pulled two tinnies out of his Esky, opened them and gave me one. "Get that into your black guts," he demanded.

And I said: "What? Are you sick or something?"

"No, you need a drink. You spend a lot of time in Collingwood – pardon, Carringbush – and barrack for

Fitzroy. You're not only Frank and Hardy but foolish as well. You need a beer."

I took a sip and Truthful continued: "Those Carringbush supporters are a mad lot. Did I ever tell you about the Collingwood barracker who went to see his team in a semi-final – on his wedding anniversary?"

"No, did he take his wife?"

"No, she supported a women's hockey team – wasn't interested in football. But she was a great celebrater. She made a big affair out of birthdays, Mother's Days, Father's Days, Xmases and New Years. But her specialty was their wedding anniversary. Always turned it on – roast dinner by candlelight, champagne, and a bit of nooky chucked in – without fail."

"Must have been quite a lady . . ."

"Was she ever – would have been a feminist except for her love of the old tossle which grew large between the legs of her football fanatic husband. 'Celebration Clara' was her name.

"Anyway, this day she gave her husband – he was called 'Fanatical Fred' – a big kiss before he left for the footie and made all sorts of sexual suggestions: a tiger in the sack was the old Clara! Fred went off rubbing his hands with glee, saying: 'Collingwood will win, no worries – and I'm on a promise from Clara!'"

"Would have been quite a night," I commented.

"Clara was really ready to celebrate in a low-cut negligee.

"But when Fanatical Fred came home he refused a drink; he even refused to respond to her kisses. In fact, he went to bed without eating a mouthful, pulled the covers over his head and went straight to sleep. Collingwood had got beaten by 10 goals!"

"Yes," I said. "They take their football seriously in Carringbush, all right."

"Not as seriously as in Chinkapook."

"Where?"

"Chinkapook! A town in the Mallee. Did I ever tell you about the violinist from Chinkapook who wanted to be a League footballer? Funny thing about Victoria: young fellas don't want to be doctors or musicians or engine drivers;

they want to be League footballers."

At that moment, the Roys ran out on to the field followed by the St Kilda team – and I managed to shut Truthful up.

After Fitzroy got beaten by some miracle, Truthful managed to drag me to a nearby pub.

# *Hardyarn*

(As told by Truthful Jones)

This bloke from Chinkapook could play the fiddle nearly as good as Yehudi Menuhin but he didn't practise much because he wanted to be a League footballer.

Lanky fella he was. Worst footballer in the district but a real good kick.

Trouble was, he couldn't get the ball to kick it. Played a few games in the local team but never got a kick, so they dropped him.

But he kept comin' to practice Tuesdays and Thursdays. Well, one day the captain of the Chinkapook Football Club got a brainwave.

He said to the selection committee, give this bloke another trial, put him in the goals. Fullback. He'll kick to the centre every time the other team scores a behind. Selection committee put him in as fullback.

The violinist never touched the ball until the last quarter. The other team kicked 16 goals straight without a behind and Chinkapook were 14 goals, seven behinds. Needed a goal to win with a few minutes to go.

Well, this violinist bloke is standing on his own in the goals. Someone kicks the ball and it hits him in the face.

He grabs it and runs for his life around the wing, where there's no players, his legs flailing like a windmill in a high wind. Bouncing the ball every few yards, he was. Frightened as a sparrow locked in a barn.

Well, he ran like a cartwheel without a rim, right up to the forward line, about 50 yards out. Easy for him from there. He was just going to kick one of his mighty punts on the run when the final bell rang. He never got another game after that."

At this point, I had asked Truthful: "I suppose he went back to the fiddle and became a world famous violinist?"

"No," Truthful replied. "Last I heard of him he had sold his violin and was running an SP book in Mildura."

# Bigger than Tex's

I wrote a book *The Unlucky Australians* about the land rights battle of the sober, sensible, Gurindji tribe, and won the Australian Yarn-Spinning Competition at the same time.

In 1966, to be exact.

There I was in Darwin trying to organise a free lift to Wattie Creek on a Darwin Administration aeroplane. This caused much delay because the Darwin Administration liked me even less that Alice Springs tiger snakes; but some of their pilots were sympathetic to the Gurindji cause and would "give me a lift", listed as a side of beef or a sack of potatoes.

They were good battlers, those pilots, because the Gurindji had occupied tribal land which, at that time, was rented by Lord Vestey for 10 cents per square mile a year.

Then one day when drinking with Rum Jungle Jack White in the Old Vic Hotel what did I see on the front page of the local newspaper? I saw a challenge from Tall-tale Tex Tyrrell himself, the acknowledged Australian yarn-spinning champion, challenging all comers to talk him out of his title.

Well, I needed the money, didn't I? So, encouraged by Rum Jungle Jack and Jim Bowditch, editor of the Northern Territory News, I accepted the challenge: the first prize was $500, a silver tray and a gold shovel.

The fact that Tall-tale Tex had boasted in the paper that he'd beaten Chips Rafferty, Morrie Amsterdam and Walkie-talkie Walker didn't bug me at all.

I could tell a yarn under water and knew 200 on the subject of horse racing alone.

Soon I met the redoubtable champion, Tall-tale Tex, himself. You'd never meet such a character in a day's walk: he was tattood from head to foot (in fact, he claimed to have tattoos on everything except the balls of his feet).

He seemed a quiet sort of chap to be a yarn-spinning champion but, after the contracts were signed, a sponsor found (Swan Breweries, naturally), Walkie-talkie Walker arrived from Alice Springs to warn me against going on with the contest.

"Tex could talk his way through an iron wall," Walker said.

"I reckon I know more yarns than he does," I replied.

"But you won't be able to tell them for long, because Tall-tale Tex's voice is so bloody monotonous that you'll yell for mercy," Walkie-talkie continued. "I could've beaten him but, after nine hours, I put me hands over me ears and told the judges to stop him for the love of Christ!"

Any doubts I had were washed away when Tall-tale Tex and I were offered free bed and lodging at the Hotel Darwin for two nights.

Swan Breweries built a platform in the main bar of the Hotel Darwin and the Alice Springs Liars Club appointed three judges including Cecil Holmes, the film director.

Points were to be allotted for the quality of the story and the way it was told.

Points were to be deducted if a filthy story was told because we were on radio. Tex and I were searched by the judges to make sure we had no notepaper carrying punch-lines or suchlike.

Sharp at noon we started. I won the toss and spoke first.

The chief judge solemnly warned me that each yarn must be of no less than one minute and no more than three.

I was well ahead on points by the afternoon teabreak.

When we started again, Tex's droning got to me.

Walkie-talkie yelled out: "You're listening to his bloody stories. Pretend you can't hear him!"

Taking Walkie-talkie's advice I forged ahead again and, some time after dark, a blank expression came over Tex's face, like that of an actor who has forgotten his lines.

He had one minute to start another yarn but his mind had gone completely blank due to drinking too much beer and listening to my stories.

Then I was declared the winner and presented with the prizes: 500 lovely Oxford scholars, a suitably inscribed silver tray and the gold shovel.

The shovel, of course, was only gold plated with cheap paint. I asked one of the judges what the shovel was for and he replied: "To shovel away all the bullshit you're going to talk for the rest of your life!"

# Hardyarn

One result of this epic battle of words was that Truthful Jones discovered a story that was funnier than any of the yarns told by me and Tex.

Loudspeakers were specially arranged outside the hotel for the competition: the bars were packed and people sat in cars outside drinking and listening.

As fate would have it, according to Truthful, during the contest a planeful of American millionaires landed at Darwin Airport because of a fault in the plane and were accommodated at the Hotel Darwin.

They were at the other end of the block from the bar where the contest was on but they could hear the yarns over the loudspeakers.

Every now and again, a local drunk would grab the microphone and broadcast a dirty Dad and Dave story, or some such.

These yarns didn't appeal to the Yankee millionaires for some reason, so the lady in charge of the tour rang the reception desk to complain about the language.

No one answered – the receptionist was down at the bar listening to the yarn-spinning contest.

So the Yankee PR lady rang the police station: "Is that the Police precinct?" she asked.

"No, it's the copper shop!" came the reply.

"Can I speak to the sergeant or whoever is in charge?" she asked politely enough.

The voice at the other end of the phone replied: "There's no coppers here; they're all over at the yarn-spinning competition."

"And who are you?"

The voice replied: "I'm in jail, but they left the door of me cell open so I could answer the phone."

If you don't believe that story, you can ask Truthful Jones himself.

# Steamroller Politics

Regular readers of *People* would know, for sure, that I have no contacts in the posh Melbourne Club; if a member saw me comin' he'd hurry across the road.

Yet, an old sparring partner of mine, Phillip Adams (Phillip who?) wrote in a newspaper column warning people against "moral crusaders" like me: "There's a theory about Frank Hardy's *Power Without Glory*, the book that blew Victoria's Labor Party apart.

"The argument goes that Frank Hardy had been fed material from sources not a hundred miles from the Melbourne Club, with the specific intention of wrecking the ALP."

I'd never heard that theory before but I wrote a letter pointing out that it was "as untrue as it is ridiculous." No material was fed to me from any Melbourne Club-type sources.

My sources were members of the Labor movement who opposed John Wren and Santamaria. And Wren-men like Sugar Roberts and Con Loughnan who were unaware that I was writing the book.

Far from wrecking the Victorian ALP, my novel helped to clear out the corrupt elements as well as the "ultra right."

The controversy brought back memories of the four years (1946-50) when I was researching and writing *Power Without Glory*.

I knew that the only way I could really find out what had gone on inside the Wren machine which controlled inner suburban Labor Party politics for 50 years was to get to know people on the inside.

Several people who had known John Wren in his heyday were still alive; there were some strange bloody characters amongst them and the strangest of them all were Sugar Roberts and Cornelius (Con) Loughnan.

To be on the safe side, I should point out that John West in my novel and the television series *Power Without Glory* was not John Wren – just a character based on certain characteristics of him.

I was introduced to Cornelius by a railway worker as Frank Rice (a name I made up on the spur of the moment). Soon Con looked on me as a mate of his and he called all his mates Doctor, for some obscure reason.

Cornelius was an absolute bottomless pit of information. He talked like a Collingwood larrikin and dressed like a Collins Street broker so you would think there was a ventriloquist in the room.

When I met him in 1946, Cornelius was on the outer with the machine because he'd worked too hot, even for John Wren, when Mayor of Richmond.

One of his mayoral exploits was to bring a middle-aged Fitzroy Street prostitute to meet the Duke of Kent as Lady Mayoress.

On another occasion, Cornelius, who was a mad punter, had a few SP bookies on his back when who should come in the door of his office at the Richmond Town Hall but a character selling steamrollers.

Now the council had a perfectly good steamroller but when the salesman offered Cornelius a commission of £2000, he decided he had to get rid of it.

Imagine the scene in the dead of night. The Mayor, with a thousand quid's worth of clothes on, finds the steamroller parked in a side street near the Yarra River. He starts it up, drives across an asphalt road, through a wire fence and jumps out before the steamroller crashes over the bank and sinks deep into the mud on the bed of the river.

Cornelius introduced me as Doctor Frank Rice to Sugar Roberts, John Wren's "fixer" in the Labor party. One of Sugar's main jobs was to ensure that men sympathetic to John Wren were elected to councils and into Parliament from suburbs like Collingwood, Richmond, Fitzroy and Carlton.

He spoke to me quite openly about how he fulfilled this task by stacking the Labor Party branches and voting in the name of people who were seriously ill or dead.

Sugar used to say: "The halt, the lame and the dead vote early and often."

In 1950, I began an "underground" printing job on *Power Without Glory* with the generous help of my old mate, George Seelaf (may you live long and die happy, "fellow slave!").

How would Sugar and Cornelius react to the novel? That thought often crossed my mind.

The problem of Sugar was solved by natural causes when the newspapers carried news of his death.

After the book was published I met Cornelius in a pub in Richmond. "How are you, Con?" I said, sounding him out.

"Not the best, Doctor," Cornelius replied. "Things are so bad I'm thinking of doing a salvage job on that bloody steamroller and selling it as scrap."

With that, Cornelius pulled a copy of *Power Without Glory* from his overcoat pocket and asked me to autograph it.

The first edition of the novel was titled *Power Without Glory by Frank Hardy ("Ross Franklyn")* – until 1950 I'd used the pen-name of Ross Franklyn, a combination of my name and that of my wife, Rosslyn (God rest your soul, "dear funny face who loved so well!")

While I autographed the book "Ross Franklyn", Cornelius said, "You're a shrewdhead, Doctor. You put two names on the book and kept your real name a secret." He went to the grave soon afterwards still believing I was Frank Rice.

Sugar and Cornelius had strong gangster leanings but they, at least, had the saving grace of a Damon Runyon-type humour and were saints compared to today's crime bosses.

# *Hardy*arn

One Saturday morning, I met Sugar Roberts in the Bendigo Hotel, Collingwood. He was all dressed up with his pockets full of Builders' Labourers Union membership receipt books (in those days only financial members of a union could vote in a Labor Party pre-selection ballot).

Sugar said there was a pre-selection ballot on that day at Carlton and he was off to write out receipts so "the halt, the lame and the dead" could vote for his man.

I went to the football at Victoria Park then returned to the pub. Just before six o'clock (closing time) Sugar arrived back.

"I've had a hard day, Doctor," he explained. "There I am on the corner writing out Builders' Labourers receipts for our men to vote on when along comes Sam Jackson and he starts writing out Timber Workers' receipts for supporters of the other candidate. Finished up with writer's cramp, I did."

I asked Sugar: "How will the ballot go?"

"Oh, our man will win," Sugar replied. "I always was a faster writer than Sam Jackson."

And so it came to pass that Sugar's man won the Labor Party pre-selection ballot for the seat of Carlton and went on to become a cabinet minister.

Oh, be on your guard, dear citizens of Australia; dreader deeds than these lie ahead of us!

# How Darwin Beat the Poms

I was in a waterfront pub in Newcastle thinking about the days long ago when Truthful Jones and I sailed out of there as seamen. And who should walk into the bar but Truthful himself.

"Goodday" he said. And I said "Goodday, what brings you back to these parts? Thinking of working on the BHP ships again?"

When I had bought a drink, Truthful asked, "And what's an Australian Rules man like you doing in Newcastle on a Saturday during the football season?"

Before I could answer, he began to talk about Rugby League, sounding off about the real and imagined skills and thrills of the game.

I decided to shut him up with the stop-start criticism of League. "Too many tackles, too many stops and starts."

"Watch it," Truthful replied, "or I'll bring up the matter of aerial ping-pong in relation to Australian Rules."

"Well," I finally admitted, "I suppose great Rugby League players would have made great Australian Rules players and vice-versa . . ."

"Some would," Truthful admitted. "Leigh Matthews of Hawthorn would have made a top League back and Johnny Raper would have made a great ruck rover.

"But Rugby League forwards would be too slow for Australian Rules as it's played today; and your Aussie Rules six-foot-eight ruckmen would be useless in League."

Truthful argued that the excitement in Rugby League arose precisely from the tackles and scrums.

"I'd call you a cupboard Rugby League man," I accused, "except I've never heard you tell a Rugby League yarn; plenty of yarns about Aussie Rules, none about Rugby . . ."

"Didn't I ever tell you how Darwin beat the England Rugby League team years ago?" Truthful took up the challenge.

"That I don't believe."

"If you don't believe me, ask Off-side Knox; he refereed.

"Well, this particular year," Truthful Jones said, "the Poms landed off the plane for a warm-up game with Darwin. They weren't very fit but they didn't worry; the First Test was three weeks off and they could beat Darwin with a one-legged team, or so they thought.

"Off-side Knox was a real patriotic Territorian. He had a plan, see. First thing he did was to send the Poms swimming."

"What good would that do?"

"Well, they was all white-skinned on account of the English weather. They swam and lay in the sun and next day they were all sunburned. Now if you've ever tried to play Rugby League with a bad sunburn, you'll know what I'm talking about."

"I reckon England could beat Darwin if all their players were blistered from head to toe."

"Not with Off-side Knox as referee, they couldn't.

"Off-side says: 'Now you fellas, I want to see a good clean game. No punching or biting off ears nor nothing like that.

"'And there's one other thing. You English players mightn't realise it yet, but the ground here is so hard you can't dig a hole for a place kick.'

"So the Pom skipper says: 'Then how will we place the ball for a penalty kick or to convert a try?'

"'You'll just have to kick punt kicks,' Off-side says. 'That'll be fair to both teams. There's just one more thing; the ground being so hard, we couldn't dig holes for goal posts, needless to say.'

"The Pom skipper was getting a bit niggly by this time. 'Listen, choom,' he says, 'we can't play without goal posts.'

"Off-side Knox says: 'We've got goal posts, all right. The only difference is that we've got blokes holding them up.'

"The game starts. No one kicks for goal in the first 10 minutes. The Poms were a bit handicapped by the sunburn.

"Just then, a Darwin player attempts a field goal. The kick is falling short but the two blokes holding the goal posts tilt them forward a bit and the ball goes over the crossbar.

"The Poms apply the pressure but Darwin holds them off until half-time. In the dressing room, the skipper says to his team: 'Listen, chooms, those goal posts moved for sure and they will move the other way if we are kicking for goal. But we'll trick 'em. We'll take the ball over for a try.'

"So he works out a special plan to get the ball to their fastest winger. At last they get the ball out to this winger and he's away, going for his life towards the line.

"Then a funny thing happens; the two blokes holding the goal posts at that end turn out to be the fastest runners in Darwin, specially picked for the job by Off-side Knox.

"And they start to run for the lick of their lives across the Botanic Gardens with the Pom winger after them carrying the ball. The goal posts kept going across the gardens towards the Fannie Bay Hotel.

"Old Off-side runs along with the Pom winger. The winger asks him: 'Where's the dead ball line?' And Off-side tells him: 'Ten yards the other side of those goal posts.'

"So the goal posts keep going and the winger gets a bit tired and some of the Darwin mob catch him before he can catch the goal posts and they tackle him good and hard.

"And every time the Poms ran for a try, the goal posts ran faster. And that's how Darwin beat the Poms."

So I said to Truthful Jones: "I'm going to Sydney to the races at Warwick Farm. Want a lift?"

"Not me. There's a big Rugby League game on here: St George versus Canberra."

"What, here in Newcastle?"

"Yeh, neutral territory."

"St George ought to win. They're on top of the League ladder," I ventured.

"Want to bet?"

Now, one thing I've learned over the years is never bet on football with Truthful Jones. So I decided to head for Sydney.

As I left the bar, Truthful said: "I'll see you later."

And I knew he would – somewhere.

# Fixing the Drug Menace

These days, the rebellion of youth takes the form of being different from the older generation: wearing different clothes, having different haircuts, listening to different music and taking different drugs.

In the '30s, the generation gap was not so wide. The dole was not paid to singles, so most young people couldn't afford different clothes or any kind of haircut. For music, they relied on the radio and they used the same drugs as their parents – alcohol and tobacco.

Under-age drinking and smoking was the go in those days: it was illegal and parents did not aprove.

The attraction of the illegal to the rebellious has always been strong.

In recent years, the youth have become a commercial target: a separate market caters for and develops their taste in clothes, music, haircuts and drugs.

This youth market includes all kinds of drugs, and sections of youth prefer illegal drugs. Beer and tobacco are "straight" drugs, used by the Oldies. If you're going to rebel and be different, you've got to try marihuana (dope or grass), cocaine (coke or snow) or heroin (smack or liquid sky).

Illegal drugs are a large segment of the youth market, and the greatest growth industry overall.

Several Royal Commissions have failed to even slow down the growth of the illegal drug market. These commissions have led to the federal government setting up a National Crimes Authority, with a specific mandate covering drugs. Now, Neville Wran proposes a NSW Drug Commission along similar lines.

To be successful, any action against the illegal drug traffic must strike at the huge rate of profit involved.

The "hard" drug market, though illegal, is a market just like that for way-out clothes or rock music. The difference lies only in the social harm done by the product – and the rate of profit.

Estimates made recently by Paul Fitzwarren, of Health Research Associates, reveal that the rate of profit on heroin is 1000 per cent; a gram of heroin has a landing price of 40¢ and a street value of $400.

Fitzwarren forecasts a profit to the heroin industry this year of $295 million, after allowing for all costs, including $8 million for bribing officials.

And where do people get the money to pay for this horrendously expensive drug? Fitzwarren estimates that, in 1984-85, money to purchase illegal drugs will be found as follows: property theft $278 million; prostitution $82 million; other illegal activities $24 million; and legal income $2 million.

Dr Robert Marks, speaking at a University of NSW conference, argued that efforts to reduce the supply of heroin through Customs seizure (in 1983, seizures totalled 97 kg) and by intensified police efforts to prevent the landed drug reaching the user, had failed.

Even steep increases in price do not seem to affect the demand for heroin, for reasons that are now obvious.

The people who read *People* have, no doubt, often pondered over this tragic problem, as I have.

Now I want to relate to them the startling conclusion I have reached. The only way to break the criminal trafficking in drugs is to legalise all drugs, including marihuana, cocaine and heroin!

Shock! Horror!

But, dear people who read *People*, think about the matter fairly and look the problem straight in the face and you will see the logic of my proposal.

If the huge profit margins were removed by the simple act of selling marihuana in tobacco shops and cocaine and heroin in chemist shops at controlled prices, the element in the community spreading and battening on the hard drug habit would soon lose interest, and drug addiction, in the long term, would be reduced to a minimum.

Dr Marks also pointed out that: "street heroin is always adulterated, sometimes with dilutants harmful to the addict

. . ." My proposal would remove the dangers of adulterated heroin, as well, of course, as the annual property theft of $278 million.

This legislation could be gradual and run parallel with the attempts to bring the dealers and the Mr Bigs behind them to book for their monstrous crimes against society.

Put another way, what I am advocating is that hard drugs should be treated the same as beer and tobacco, which are also demonstrably harmful to the health and social well-being of the community.

Drug addiction arises from the very fabric of society, and the legalisation of all drugs would enable society to combat the use of drugs by programs of education.

# *Hardyarn*

Even if you've heard this yarn before, it is nonetheless appropriate to the occasion.

A bush horse trainer became convinced that his horses were losing because city trainers were using speed-up dope when he raced against their horses. So he approached the local chemist and persuaded him to make up some dope in the form of lumps of sugar.

At the track the trainer gave his horse three lumps. At that vital moment, a city steward came from behind a tree and asked: "What did you administer to that animal?"

"Only a few harmless lumps of sugar, Your Worship!"

The steward replied: "If it's so harmless, let me see you eat a lump!"

The bush trainer obliged by chewing a lump of sugar and stuffed one into the mouth of the city steward.

As he legged the jockey up, the trainer muttered: "This is a certainty! Take it to the front, and if you hear anything coming behind yer, don't worry – it'll be me or the city steward!"

The moral of this story is that if drugs were legal and used on all horses, the situation would find its own level and all trainers would stop using drugs.

102

# Legalise Drugs to Hit at the Mr Bigs

One Friday night, the Prime Minister and the Premiers of all the states of Australia went on TV to tell the people of Austalia something they had known for many years: that the drug menace was out of control and something must be done about it.

The Prime Minister quoted some frightening statistics about drug-related death and crime: 20 per cent of all deaths of people between 20 and 34 were drug-related, and the majority of robberies committed were drug-related.

A brochure was to be issued to every household in Australia to attempt to educate people about the drug menace.

On the list of priorities, law enforcement was last.

Of course, this campaign and the establishment of a national crimes authority could be a big step forward in combating the drug menace, which threatens the fabric of the Australian way of life, but is this campaign just another piece of vote-catching?

On the ABC program, *Four Corners,* the extent of the drug menace was traced by interviewing heroin victims and showing how readily available hard drugs were, not only in Kings Cross and St Kilda, but in every suburb and town throughout the country.

*Four Corners* announced that the Prime Minister, the Premiers and the National Crimes Authority had refused invitations to appear and be questioned about the new campaign.

In their place, *Four Corners* interviewed the four gentlemen who had conducted Royal Commissions into organised crime and drugs in the past 15 years, including Justice Stewart, the first Royal Commissioner into organised crime and Frank Costigan, the latest.

They reckoned politicians of all parties lacked the political will to carry through a vigorous campaign against organised crime and drugs.

Their main criticism was that the National Crimes Authority was a toothless tiger because many of the state crime authorities did not co-operate sufficiently.

Their other criticism was that recommendations made in four separate inquiries had not been followed through.

Frank Costigan's inquiry was cut short. He was bitterly attacked in public and the recommendations of his report were virtually ignored.

One judge said at least this campaign was a step in the right direction and he hoped the National Crimes Authority would be given the powers it needed to enforce the law against the monsters who are spreading drugs throughout this community like poisoned gas.

But the people who read *People*, the ordinary man and woman in the street, were not so sure.

More than 70 per cent of them said a couple of weeks later that they thought the plan would not work.

Rev. Ted Noffs said: "It's a waste of money!"

The famous rock singer, Sting, commented: "The thing is to stop young people from thinking it's hip to take hard drugs; and if a Prime Minister says it's not hip, then the young people are apt to say it is."

Sting seemed to think that most young people would take no notice of what the Prime Minister said or wrote.

Of course the campaign of educating people may lead to some reduction but in the end, it's a matter of stopping the supply.

This is where governments seem to have failed.

In the 15 years since the first Royal Commission, story after story has appeared in the newspapers and on TV about corruption in high places in relation to the Mr Bigs of organised crime.

My impression is that there has been some improvement in the past year. In NSW, for example, more than 100 police officers are facing charges of corruption.

But has this corruption become a way of life?

Is your friendly street corner pusher merely practising private enterprise? One of the heroin addicts interviewed on TV said people in the scene never call such people pushers.

They just seem to think that they are ordinary people selling hammer (as they call heroin). But sometimes the pushers pretend to have no marihuana or cocaine, only hammer in order to create another addict.

One young woman said that if she could motivate herself for any other job or any other career the way she motivated herself to commit robberies to score hammer, then she could do anything.

One of the judges said: "There will always be a supply of hard drugs while there are profits to be made. We have to ask ourselves why there is such a large demand for drugs."

I agree with the first statement: that there will always be a supply while there's a fortune to be made out of them.

Drug peddling is now the biggest industry in Australia and the rate of profit in it is by far the highest of any industry. But the judge failed to see that supply and demand are closely linked.

Most pushers have developed an expensive drug habit themselves and sell drugs to other people – even to children – to feed their own habits. The Mr Bigs just sit up there somewhere in the mysterious rapture world, laughing all the way to the bank to launder their money.

Only two ways can be found to cut off the supply – and slash demand.

They are: enforcement with such honesty and even savagery, including phone tapping of criminals and corrupt officials, to make this horrendous heroin trade the most dangerous occupation on earth. Or alternatively: to make all drugs legal, as I've said before.

Shock! Horror! But I urge you to think about it. Marihuana should be legalised first.

And then the harder hard drugs, even hammer!

And people who are still determined to get it can simply say to their doctor: "I've got a heroin habit: I want a prescription."

They would then go to the chemist's shop where heroin would only be a very small fraction of its present street price.

So either put up or shut up!

Either root out the Mr Bigs behind the drug trade or legalise all drugs and so take the profit out of selling them.

All the public education in the world will not solve the problem unless one of the alternatives above are adopted.

# *Hardyarn*

Speaking of dope and drugs reminds me of the late Huck Finlay, the Queensland jockey, who had a stammer.

One day a trainer suggested to Huck that they should give a certain horse a speed-up drug. "B-be no use," Huck replied. "He'd only go to sleep."

"Well, what about a battery?" the trainer asked.

Just at that moment, an aeroplane was going over, so Huck said: "No use hitting him with a j-j-jigger. He couldn't win a race with an engine of that b-b-bloody plane tied to his tail."

On another occasion, Huck won a race on a 100-to-1 shot and he went around all the bookmakers with an old hat asking for donations.

Huck Finlay was renowned as a rider of front runners.

When he died, the hearse at the head of the funeral was passing a pub when a drinker yelled out: "Good luck to you, Huck! You always were at your best out in front."

# It's Only Money – Or Is It?

Money replaced barter as a means of exchange. Coins eventually became the currency of nations: bronze, silver and, eventually, gold.

At the time of Jesus Christ, there were already money changers in the temple.

The modern banking system replaced metal coins with cheques – in the greatest confidence trick in history. Money became paper! It was used to create credit, to make profit on paper. To make profit without selling anything is theft.

Is money theft?

Paper money was invented nearly 400 years ago. At first, it had to be backed by its equivalent in metal coins, eventually by its equivalent in gold.

Now, money has only the backing of paper. Paper has become collateral for the loan of paper. It would be funny to say that paper is as valuable as gold: paper money is "funny money".

Turning money into the theft of credit creation was invented by a Dutchman in 1609. He broke the law which said that money must be backed by metal. He loaned money by book entry. He handed out four times as much money on paper as he held in coins.

He ended up in jail, but the practice of loaning out more than the amount held in metal became commonplace in the banking system.

A banker, using non-legal tender, gets 15 per cent; a forger, using non-legal tender, gets 15 years. A banker is a forger with an office!

Metal money was largely replaced by cheques – and banks continued to lend money they didn't have. Hungry for higher interest rates, they formed finance and hire purchase companies to which they sent their less well-heeled customers without collateral to be charged exhorbitant interest rates.

These finance companies are said to be "good sports with money" – but try owing them $10,000!

The goods hired have become the collateral. The finance companies, like the banks who own them, possess only a fraction of the money they loan on paper.

Now money, like gold, is going out of fashion. Coins and paper money are used for only small transactions.

Paper money and coins have been largely replaced by plastic. Plastic money has many different names: Bankcard, Diners Club, American Express. The latest fad is a plastic card which you insert in a slot in a bank wall and press a computer code. Hey presto! The money coughs out!

Plastic money has become an obsession. Oh, dear people who read *People,* take a gander at the plastic people with plastic money: you'll see them standing outside a bank, waiting to insert their Handybank card, while tellers stand idle inside the bank waiting to serve them more quickly.

Exorbitant rates are charged for this dubious honour. Anyone without a plastic card is now viewed with considerable suspicion.

I first noticed this 10 years ago in London. I booked into a Holiday Inn without a credit card. The receptionist eyed me with an icy glare as if I were an escaped convict (they were employing mainly ex-warders from Dachau at that time). Something wrong here: this mug wants to pay cash! She demanded a day's tariff in advance and said I would have to pay in advance every day.

Just to give them the horrors, I would sneak in and out until I owed them a few hundred quid.

Returning to the pub one night late, I was dropped off by David Frost (I was doing business with him then, God help me). The night receptionist confronted me to say that unless I paid up to date, my room would be let.

I dived out the door and managed to catch David before he drove away. He came in with his plastic smile to open a folding wallet full of credit cards: "Which one do you want?"

When he had gone, the lady, Elsa Kosch, I think her name was, reluctantly allowed me to stay. "We don't trust people without credit cards," she informed me.

The Holiday Inn was owned by the Baptist Church. The Bible by your bed was open at a different page every day. Next morning, I found my Bible open at the page telling the story of the honest servant who always paid his debts!

These days, plastic money rules the fashionable pubs: you can't get in without a credit card. Oh, for the good old days when you could book into a pub and pay as you left!

And you can't hire a car without a credit card. I tried recently in Sydney. "No credit card, no car," the man said. I had a few hundred dollars in cash. "No use, the car is worth thousands."

So money has gone full circle: bronze and silver money became gold; gold became paper; and paper became plastic. All of which was designed to conceal the fact that the financial institutions do not have the money they lend you.

The same situation applies to the loan of money by the International Monetary Fund to the poor nations. On behalf of mainly American banks, the International Monetary Fund, for example, loaned Bolivia $72 billion. It now loans them money to pay the interest on the interest – and the banks didn't have the money in the first place!

Last month, seven more American banks closed their doors, making a total of 43 since the beginning of the year. These, of course, are small banks. When, in February, one of the major American banks was going to the wall, Uncle Sam had to rescue it.

Most of these banks went broke simply because the depositors, hearing rumours, asked for their money and the banks didn't have it.

And yet, the plastic people push their plastic money into a slot in a bank wall, believing that all is well.

# *Hardy*arn

Truthful Jones' definition of money: "Money is a poor man's credit card."

# Ball and Chain Humour

You can't win – but you've got to battle. That is the basis and essence of Australian humour.

At least, that's how artist Vane LIndesay worked it out donkey's years ago when we were working together as artists on the army journal *Salt*.

Vane and I are convinced that there is a peculiarly Australian humour and that its main theme is the battler, the loser trying to get in front. Male or female, they battle against the odds.

Probably this strange basis for our humour is due to our convict origins and pioneer beginnings. You really did have to battle with a ball and chain around your ankles in the convict days – just to survive.

And you really did have to battle when you headed inland seeking the unknown in the great continent. (If only more of those pioneers had realised that the Australian Aborigine is also a battler – in fact, he is the ultimate battler.)

I once wrote a song, which some of the people who read *People* will remember, called *Sydney Town*. This was based on the theme of the Australian battler. It began:

Great grandaddy walked along the street,
with a ball and chain around his feet,
and that's the way they want to see me walk,
just to give the toffs a chance to talk.

In each stanza this battler really thinks he's got the system beaten but you know it's just the old story: he can't win but he has to keep battling.

And ended:

The capitalists they got it all arranged
They buy their shares on the stock exchange
But I bought some tickets with me spouse
And we got shares in the Opera House.

That song was number two on the hit parade and ready to

go into the top slot when what should bloody happen? The Beatles released a record called *Help* and it went to number one in the first week!

Ned Kelly was the first Aussie battler. Got killed before he was 25 and became a national hero.

No one will be surprised to learn that my latest book is about losers who battle. It's called *The Loser Now Will Be Later To Win*.

There are 10 long short stories, beginning in 1895 with that story of Henry Lawson and Victor Daley touching Archibald of the *Bulletin* for 50 quid to bury Lawson 25 years before he died and ending with a story set in Footscray in 1985.

The title of the book comes from Bob Dylan's song *The Times They Are A-Changing*.

"Don't speak too soon for the wheel's still in spin and there's no telling who that it's naming, for the loser now will be later to win, for the times they are a-changing."

As a battler from way back, I am convinced that your typical Australian is in fact the Aussie Battler – not the Ocker!

The Australian battler is usually an honest enough fellow – but he might sell you something that dropped off the back of a truck.

One such battler was a character on the Sydney waterfront named Honest Hambone.

The waterfront detectives used to lie awake at night thinking up ways to catch Honest Hambone.

One time a shipment of chiming clocks came in from Switzerland. The Lollipops reckoned the old Hambone wouldn't be able to resist such a charming gift.

So they went down the hold in the middle of the night and set all the chiming clocks to go off at five o'clock – Brahms' Lullaby. At five o'clock you'd think there was a symphony orchestra playing as the wharfies came off the day shift.

So the Ds grab Honest Hambone and search his bag but it was empty.

While they were searching Hambone, about a dozen wharfies went through the gate to the accompaniment of Brahms' Lullaby.

Well, one night the waterfront detectives are standing at the gate chewing the rag about not being able to catch Honest Hambone when he choofs along wheeling a barrow full of straw. The coppers rub their hands with glee.

They search through the straw and under it. But the wheelbarrow was empty. Next night, up choofs old Honest Hambone again wheeling his barrow full of straw. They search it again, but it's empty.

They're suspicious, see, so they have a conference with the Customs officials and decide to examine the wheelbarrow. They turn it over. Pull the bottom off it to see if it was false, but found nothing. They even poked a stick down the hollow of the handlebars.

They were going round the bend and one of the detectives says to Honest H.: "Listen, we know you're the biggest thief on the waterfront. If we promise not to book you, will you tell us what you're stealing?"

Now, Hambone had been brought up never to trust a policeman so he says to one of the Customs officials: "If I tell you, you'll promise not to book me?"

"Cross me heart and hope to die," the Customs man says pleading.

"Barrows," Hambone told them. "There's a shipment being unloaded at number seven wharf."

# Soup Kitchen Barbs

There we were, the unemployed and the unemployable, standing in the foyer of the National Art Gallery, Canberra, on the Monday of the tax summit waiting for the guests to arrive for the banquet: tycoons, politicians, trade union officials and the welfare people.

Who was unemployable? Me! The old F.J. Hardy himself, who hasn't done an honest day's work since 1966 when he worked with a shovel in the stockhold of a BHP ship sailing out of Newcastle, that's who.

And who were the unemployed? They were out of work people and pensioners who had lived below the poverty line for a long time. Most of them had slept in a tent on the lawn in front of Parliament House the night before, when the temperature was two degrees below bloody zero.

All of them, young and old, were very employable – except that there are no jobs for them in the lucky country because the capitalists won't invest unless they can make super profits.

And was Hardy, the most Australian Australian, sucking up to the silvertails, waiting for crumbs from their banquet table? Not on your bloody life, he wasn't. He was eating tomato soup from the soup kitchen the unemployed had set up in the plush foyer.

We had come from Melbourne, Sydney, Wollongong and Brisbane in our hundreds, under the banner of The Coalition Against Poverty and Unemployment. We had little money to pay for buses and other expenses; we were representing tens of thousands.

The farmers had come in their tens of thousands that morning. Some of them had money even for aeroplanes. They were representing millions.

Watch yourselves, you leaders of the people and you Pitt Street millionaires, your system has reduced the country towns of Australia to what Doug Anthony himself called ghettos of poverty, and the small working farmer to the brink of bankruptcy.

At first, some of the farmers resented our presence and wanted us to dismantle our big tent. It was their day, they said.

But Harry Van Morst, president of the Coalition in Melbourne, soon convinced the farmers that ours was a common cause; we too were opposed to the broad-based consumption tax, which would mean for them further rises in petrol prices; and they, like the poor in the towns and cities, would have to pay the higher prices for essential goods.

Soon farmers were coming into our tent for a cup of tea or coffee, the wiry men and the staunch women who till the soil of this land.

The farmers' leaders told us they were non-party political and that they were crook on the National Party federal leadership. In contradiction, some of the farmers were clearly supporters of Joh Bjelke-Petersen (never underestimate the cunning of Peanut Joh!).

The Coalition itself is all in the name: it is a coalition of individuals and affiliated groups which places an umbrella of efficient kindness over organisations which aim to help the poor.

It does not replace, but tries to enhance, the work of the Salvos, the refuges, the CYSS, the Right to Work, et al; and it supplies pamphlets, leaflets and newsletters which help keep the isolated groups in touch with each other.

I was a member of the Coalition in Melbourne and am now helping to form it in Sydney and country areas. I wish it were not needed but I am angry that in a land so young and fair, three million people, including 800,000 children, live on the brink of starvation and in a nightmare of doubt and debt.

Oh, dear people who read *People*, whether you are poor or not so poor, help the Coalition!

In Canberra, I made sarcastic jokes, sending up each person who arrived, while in the background the unemployed chanted: "Tax the rich!"

Reactions varied: Laurie Carmichael, of the Metal Union,

came over to me, and I asked him: "What are you doing, going in there?"

"Doing my best," he replied, and seemed a little bewildered when Lyn Dennertein asked: "For whom?" He escaped with good grace, saying, "I'm all for taxing the rich."

Mike Fitzpatrick, former Carlton football captain, came over and drank a few mouthfuls of soup without relish. Phillip Adams grinned and gave an "Up You" sign when I told him over the microphone that the Summit was going to foul up the film industry.

The big business moguls scowled when I called them "benighted wretches". Some trade union officials ducked for cover.

Bob Hawke pretended not to hear when I said: "I've got a tip for you, Bob. Scratch Keating in the Canberra Handicap!"

Peter Hollingsworth, that fine man from the Brotherhood of St Laurence, came over to us and said they were well aware of our presence, and he and some of the other welfare people, plus Neville Wran, were fighting against the tax on food and other necessities.

Some of my taunts raised laughs and I like to feel that, having thus alienated myself from the most powerful people in the country, my off-the-cuff commentary might have given them cause to stop and think.

# *Hardyarn*

Truthful Jones had a mate called Larry the Loafer. He was the greatest sponger ever God put breath in, smoked only other people's, never shouted except for help, took a cut lunch to the races, held the lantern while his mother cut the wood, and ran up a bill with Truthful's SP bookie.

He was so mean, he thought a good turn was a well-banked bend in the Pacific Highway.

Not long before Larry died of a mean heart, I said to Truthful: "Why do you put up with the bastard? He couldn't lay straight in bed and he's bludged on you for years."

"One thing I will say for the old Larry," Truthful replied, with a sly grin. "He never runs a man down behind his back. Anyway, not to worry: I claim for him as a dependent in my income tax."

# Dame Edna Average?

Here we are in Sydney's Carringbush Hotel. "I see Barry Humphries has been back in Australia," says I to Truthful Jones.

"Yeh, I saw it on TV," Truthful replied, emptying his glass in a manner that indicated he might be getting on to one of his pet hates.

"You mean when he came on as Dame Edna Everage?" I asked, hurrying to refill our glasses.

"Yeh, as if Australian women haven't got enough troubles without that galah goin' around treating them as if they were all oafs like himself. The finest women in the world, from the pioneers right up to the present day heroines, who are bringing up about half the children of this country on their own – have been abandoned by some bastard too miserable to dub in the upkeep of his own kid."

I decided to play devil's advocate. "Well, you must admit he made some very funny cracks, like the one about it costing her more to keep her husband, Norm, on the planet than it costs the Yanks to put a satellite off the planet."

Jill, one of the owners of the pub acting as barmaid, put down the drinks and said: "You're right, Truthful, I never met an Australian woman who looked or behaved like Edna Everage. This one is on the house. That man must hate women."

Thus encouraged, Truthful continued. "Hates the whole bloody human race, if you ask me.

"I usta live in Moonee Ponds and I never met no Edna Everages or the likes of Sandy Stone.

"He also invented the Ocker, because the main people he's crook on are the people who work hard for their living, and love their drop of beer, like meself."

He looked at me slyly, and added: "Admittedly, I gave up work years ago because, when I wanted work badly, THEY wouldn't give me any, so they can shove their job creation schemes up the part of Keating where the bird of paradise flew . . ."

"By Ocker, you mean Barry McKenzie?" I asked Truthful, sensing that he was about to theorise on the human condition.

"Barry McKenzie is the greatest slanderer of Australia's workin' class since Bob Menzies.

"Menzies called 'em yahoos; Humphries calls 'em Ockers.

"The Ocker is a view of the working man that comes from the effete middle class. Your Ocker is the Australian Battler, who digs the coal, drives the trains, tills the soil, demands a fair go for his mate."

He looked at Jill, who was still listening, as if heading off some possible criticism. "The term Ocker covers women as well as men – and some of the best mates I ever had were women.

"Your Ocker likes to read a good book, march in the odd demonstration and tell Them up there to get stuffed, from time to time, just to try and keep 'em honest."

"I know a few women who are crook on Ockers," I argued. "Reckon the Ocker is insensitive and doesn't always treat women properly." And I was thinking: I've got the old Truthful over a barrel here.

Without batting an eyelid, Truthful thumbed his hat back from his forehead. "Australian men and women will work

117

out their problems without any help from Barry bloody Humphries. He spreads that idea, as if only the foppish upper classes know how to relate to women."

He laughed his satirical laugh. "They know how to treat 'em, all right! Most of 'em have got a wife, won't employ a secretary unless she'll go to bed with 'im, and 'ave a mistress on the side!

"Whereas your working man or woman are more loyal to each other. Many an Ocker man writes poems for his lady, and many an Ocker woman becomes a feminist without startin' out by hatin' her 'usband . . ."

Truthful smiled at Jill. "I'm a feminist meself, because I believe in equal rights and equal bloody pay for women.

"But I'm not into spreadin' animosity between the sexes, because the battlers of this country, men and women, have got to stick together."

Thinking Truthful might be going a shade too far, as usual, I recalled: "Humphries used to be a brilliant practical joker in his young days. History has it that he and my sister Mary . . ."

Truthful interrupted: "Poor Mary, as if she didn't have enough troubles without Barry Humphries!"

"That was in his young days; they were good pals. The story goes that one of their jokes was to get on a tram in Melbourne, with Mary wearing a calliper on one of her legs, as if she was crippled, and Barry would get on, kick her on the crook leg, then get off again.

"The joke, according to Barry, was that no-one ever interrupted or tried to stop him . . ."

"Typical," Truthful said. "It's like I told yer, Humphries is crook on the whole human race.

"Do yer remember when we usta go to the races with Clipboard Gerry? Well, that long, skinny bloke with the trendy clothes, the lawyer who worked for Gerry, was high up in the Young Liberals . . ."

Truthful knew he had me. "And that selfsame leading light of the Young Liberals told me once coming home from Flemington, that nearly every branch of the Young Liberals had made group bookings to see Barry Humphries. Love to see him knocking the Ockers, did the Young Liberals . . ."

# Whose IDea is This?

I was surprised to learn that the first Gallup Polls on the ID Card rort showed about 73 per cent of Australians favoured it.

But some dag said that the plastic Prime Minister once had 73 per cent support; now only a minority support him.

Apart from the fact that I'll end up in serious bother if ever it's introduced, I'm opposed to the bloody thing on principle.

Public meetings have been held in most capital cities explaining all its implications. One of them, in Sydney, displayed that Aussie brilliance for naming organisations with words whose initial letters make sense, by calling a meeting of PAID – they'd called their organisation People Against ID.

The reason given by "Robbing Hood" Keating for ID cards is that they will prevent tax evasion.

ID cards would have no effect on the major area of tax evasion which is in the corporate company tax area.

There is no evidence that ID cards can, will, or do stop tax evasions in the few countries where they are in use.

Low income people have the most contact with government departments and will be obliged more often to present their cards. ID card holders will have no say about what information is given to that department.

Already data linkage programs have been computerised by the loan sharks. By pressing a few keys on a computer, they can bring up the credit rating of every poor bastard who ever borrowed a penny or bought anything on hire purchase.

More recently, landlords and estate agents have begun a National Tenancy Register, which provides a centralised computer and a Tenancy Card which you'll have to produce before you can rent a house or a flat.

Soon after the introduction of ID cards, the finance sharks and the landlords are bound to add your ID card number to their computer systems. So you will have government departments and huge corporations and landlords in possession of every essential detail of every citizen.

Computer matching programs will place everybody under surveillance.

In Canada, for example, people have to disclose their Social Insurance Number when cashing cheques, borrowing books from a library, renting an apartment or even enrolling in an amateur sports club!

The bureaucrats in Australia might even change the locks on public toilets so you'd have to use your plastic ID card to have an Edgar Britt!

But my main beef against the ID card is that it will rob the poor of the few lurks they still have.

The newspapers have carried stories recently which give some idea of what will happen when the ID card hits the fan. One paper reported that "falsifying identities will bring penalties for the first offender of $5000 and/or 12 months' jail, as well as doubling the tax avoided. These offences include undeclared different names for bank accounts or part-time jobs."

Hands up any battler on the dole or a pension who hasn't from time to time taken a few hours' work to stave off starvation! Well, the ID card will put an end to all that, while the big thieves with the big perks, the bottom of the harbour bludgers, will go scot-free and continue to pay little or no tax.

Surprise! Surprise! Women are likely to be harder hit than men by the ID card racket. Bloody near half the kids in Australia are being brought up by women on their own; 800,000 of their kids are living below the poverty line, in spite of the fact that some of the mothers do a little part-time work in the "cash economy."

Enough said?

# Hardyarn

The only place where the ID card might be justified is on the Wellington waterfront – practically everyone working there has a nickname, and even best mates can rarely remember their surname!

Like the story of two mates: the Smiling Seagull and the Kaiwharawhara Murderer (the latter got his name 'cos he lived in Kaiwharawhara and often said when angry, "I'll murder that so-and-so!").

Well, during World War II, these two characters worked on the Wellington waterfront and every wharfie had to have an ID card.

One day they arrived at the gate, and a copper says: "Where's yer ID card?"

The Seagull said he'd left his at home, and the copper got technical and wouldn't let him in to start work.

Pretty soon the old Murderer himself choofs along.

The Seagull starts smiling again. "Here comes me mate," he says, "he'll vouch for me."

"Do you know this man?" the constable asks the Murderer.

Says the Murderer, "Known him all me life. He's me best mate."

The copper says, "He hasn't got his ticket. What's his name?"

"Name?" the Murderer says. "His NAME?" A blank look comes over his face and he scratches his head. "Jack – er – Bill . . . it's ridiculous, I went to school with him. His name is, er . . . the Seagull, the Smiling Seagull."

"Where's YOUR ticket?" the constable asked the Murderer.

Well, the Murderer had left his ticket in his coat on the wharf.

The copper called the Seagull aside. "You claim this man has known you all his life. What's HIS name?"

The Seagull smiled again. "His name?" he said, "You're asking me his name? Listen, he's my mate."

"Well, just tell me his name."

"His NAME? Er, Bill, Tom, Ernie . . . Just a minute – it's on the tip of me tongue . . . Aw heck – the Kaiwharawhara

Murderer, that's who he is. We call him the Murderer for short."

"Why do you call him the Murderer?"

The Seagull smiled widely: "Because he's always murderin' someone."

The policeman got his book out: "There was a woman murdered at Kaiwharawhara last week."

The old Seagull couldn't resist a joke at his mate's expense. "Ah, me mate would have killed her – he's got a private cemetery out there."

The policeman said sternly, "I'm afraid you two will have to accompany me to the station."

On the way to the police station the Murderer says, "Here's the chief timekeeper. He'll vouch for us."

So the copper said to this timekeeper: "Do you know these two men? What are their names, sir?"

"Names? Everybody knows their names. The Kaiwharawhara Murderer and the Smiling Seagull!"

The policeman took the Murderer and the Seagull to the police station.

The Murderer said: "Take me to the Senior Sergeant, I know him."

The constable said: "Wait until I tell the Senior Sergeant that you two say you can vouch for each other but you don't know each other's names and one of you claims the other is a murderer!"

They eventually got to the Senior Sergeant's office. "Excuse me, sir," the constable said, "these two men claim they are wharf labourers, but they have no tickets . . ."

The Senior Sergeant laughed. "Ah, they're all right. Everybody knows them. They're the Kaiwharawhara Murderer and the Smiling Seagull!"

Which only goes to show that ID cards aren't worth the plastic they're written on!

# Scratch This for a Joke

Your genuine Aussie punter gambles mainly on horses. Horses were important to this nation's development, so it is part of our tradition, but that's not the only reason.

Your real gambler likes to get some choice, some value for his money, and some real chance of winning.

Apart from two-up, an even money bet – and our national game, which is illegal, except in legal casinos – backing horses or dogs is the best value for money that gambling offers.

You dyed-in-the-wool punters rarely Go Lotto or buy lottery tickets, and never, but never, buy Magic Money Scratchit tickets!

Gangster Al Capone, who made a lot of his money battening on the poor with the numbers racket (the then illegal American equivalent of our lottos), was a gentleman compared with the state lotteries offices which conduct the Scratchit racket.

The actor who played Squizzy Taylor in the film does the TV ads for Scratchits: "You just scratch, scratch, scratch, all you need is three symbols to match . . . win up to $25,000 . . ."

In the past two years I have found myself breaking the punter's golden rule: look for value and you'll never buy a Scratchit ticket.

I would sneak into the newsagent's shop, buy a paper and take some of the change in a Scratchit ticket – kind of like a secret drinker, sneaking the wine bottle out of the cupboard.

I did it in Melbourne, Sydney, Murwillumbah and Brunswick Heads. If, by a miracle, I won a $2 prize, I'd buy two more tickets – and lose – and so spend $3.30.

My newspapers began to become bloody expensive, so I scratched me head and studied the matter fairly . . . I would ask the newsagent, casual like: "Did you ever sell a $25,000 prize, or a $10,000 . . . or a $1000 . . .?"

Never met one who even claimed he had – but they usually knew a newsagent at Byron Bay, Collingwood or Timbuktoo who actually had. Have you ever known anyone who won the big prize on a Scratchit ticket?

Finally I asked a newsagent in Sydney if the big prize winners were ever announced. He said he thought they were – in the newspapers.

"Which newspaper, on which day?" I asked. He didn't know – but gave me a brochure with the dubious heading "Follow The Bunny To Win Magic Money!" And in it, right from the bunny's mouth, so to speak, I discovered what bloody bunnies we buyers of Scratchit tickets really are.

The bunny brochure brazenly said:

"Good luck and happy scratching. Magic money prize structure – the full prize structure for each batch of 480,000 tickets sold is: 1 x $25,000, 1 x $10,000, 2 x $1,000, 30 x $100, 60 x $50, 500 x $10, 19,000 x $5, 79,750 x $2. There are 99,344 prizes."

Get your calculators out, dear people who read *People*, and I'll show you why you should never buy another Scratchit ticket as long as you may live.

Take a gander at the above list of prizes!

For $1 (plus 10 cents commission) you have 79,750 chances of winning a $2 prize, out of 480,000! Work it out! You're paying about 6 to 1 on an even money bet! And the further up the scale you go, the worse and the more outrageous the odds against you become!

Follow me with your calculator. You have only a 25/1 chance of winning $5 for your dollar; a 960/1 chance of winning $10; an 8000/1 chance of winning $50; a 19,000/1 chance of winning $100; a 240,000/1 chance of winning $500, and no less than a 480,000/1 chance of winning either $10,000 or $25,000 for your dollar!

Scratch your head – and think! Don't Scratch, don't Go Lotto and don't buy Lottery tickets; if you must have a ticket, buy one in the "four legged lottery" (horse racing).

Next time you are tempted to buy a Scratchit ticket, go to the nearest TAB instead, and put your dollar on a horse at about even money (one in three of them wins on average); or put it on a 5/1 shot or a 10/1 shot, and so on (your chances of winning on the TAB are astronomically higher than on Scratchit).

Or better still, go to your corner store and buy a loaf of bread or a bar of chocolate – instead of that bogus Scratchit ticket.

## *Hardyarn*

The late Larry the Loafer, one-time mate of Truthful Jones, joined Gamblers Anonymous.

Truthful said to him: "You'll never make it for even a month."

Larry the Loafer retorted: "I'll bet you $500 I do!"

A month later Larry rang up Gamblers Anonymous.

"Do you want to join?" the Gamblers Anonymousman asked.

"No, I want to resign!" Larry replied. "I just won $500 off me mate!"

# The Great Australian Lover

There I was, drinking with Truthful Jones in the Carringbush Hotel, when the Sex Problem came up.

"There's more said and written about sex than football in this town," Truthful said.

"Sex is important," I defended.

"Of course it's important, but the old Henry Lawson himself summed it up; he reckoned you shouldn't make a problem of love – you should just make it.

"In every bloody magazine you pick up, you'll find articles on the Sex Problem – and sex gadgets; orgasms, real and contrived, vibrators, G-spots, foreplay and after-play, decorated condoms, single bars and double sex . . ."

I interrupted Truthful: "They reckon the trouble is that Australian men are afraid to express emotion and love . . ."

Truthful emptied his glass. "They wouldn't know. The trouble is that Australian men – and women – are encouraged to study sex as if it had nothing to do with love and emotion, like they were gymnasts . . ." Truthful looked at me slyly. "It's a thirsty subject, this . . ."

I took the hint and ordered two beers. "Some Australian women complain about Australian men and their attitude to sex, y'know, Truthful."

Truthful sipped his beer. "I never had any complaints. And you reckon you can outscrew as well as outwrite men half your age – so you couldn't have had any complaints either.

"The Sex Problem in Australia is not the men's fault and it's not the women's fault, it's history's fault.

"Yer see, in the olden days men went away droving cattle, fencing, shearing, and the women were left alone on some small farm, runnin' it and lookin' after the kids. The women and the men were separated. And that's when I reckon men got their ballsed-up ideas about women.

"A woman was either a wonderful wife at home waiting for you while you travelled around earning a living, or she was a whore in some shanty.

"It takes a long time to overcome an attitude like that. Some Australian men still want their women to be angels, but they forget to try to be saints.

"Women were at a great disadvantage in this country, and the sexual revolution didn't help them much; male chauvinism took on a new guise. But that's all in the past now. And I'm one of the pioneers who changed it . . . "

Truthful Jones glanced at me. I sensed he was in full flight on a subject he didn't often discuss, the Sex Problem. Truthful continued – when he saw me order another beer.

"Y'see, more than 20 years ago I decided to send up Australian men and their attitude to love and sex. I made up a lotta yarns and told them, and some of them even got on television and into the newspapers. One was called 'The Great Australian Lover'. A satire on Australian men.

"The Great Australian Lover's name was Curly, who had a bald head. His mate's name was Burly, who would have weighed about 30kg wringing wet in an Army overcoat with house bricks in the pockets.

"The subject of marriage came up between them in the pub one Saturday morning . . .

"'You get married today, don't yer, Curly?' Burly asked, looking up from his form guides. 'Next Saturday,' replied Curly. After some debate, Burly reckoned, 'It's terday, Curl, at noon. We've just got time to catch the first at the TAB before you go to the barrier for the Mug's Stakes.'

"The TAB queue was long, and so was the wait at the church for the bride, who was dressed in white, and her parents, who had travelled 1000km specially for the occasion.

"During the ceremony, Curly's mother-in-law-to-be got technical and commented that the groom and best man should have worn suits instead of shorts, T-shirts and thongs."

"The bride's mother was a bit narrowminded, eh?" I urged Truthful Jones on.

"The bride's father was just as bad; he asked where the reception would be held. 'Ah, we'll go over to the pub lounge and have beer and pies,' Curly told him.

"The bride's parents didn't stay long. Anyway, Curly and Burly filled the boot of their bomb with stubbies of beer for a party to celebrate the solemn occasion. All their mates came; some brought wives or sheilas. The bride came, too. The men stood at one end of the room telling dirty yarns; at the other, the women talked about what drongos their menfolk were.

"There were quite a few fights, a drinking contest and a fair bit of chundering. The bride, who was also inclined to be narrowminded, started to cry for some reason, and locked herself in the bedroom.

"When Curly woke up with roadmap eyes and a mouth like the bottom of a cocky's cage, he was under the kitchen table. Burly was on the sofa. 'Musta been quite a party,' Curly said, surveying the empty bottles and full bodies on the floor. 'What was it in aid of?' 'You got married,' Burly said. 'Where's the bride, then?' asked Curly. 'In the bedroom, a bit upset.'

"Curly knocked on the bedroom door and paled when a woman's voice answered: 'Go away. I never want to see you again.' 'Ah, come on darl, we'll 'ave to go on the honeymoon, won't we?' 'Where are we going?' the bride asked Curly. 'Hayman Island,' Curly replied, and this brought the bride out. 'I got three tickets.' 'What do we want three for?' 'Well, Burly's coming with us. He's me mate.' 'If he comes, I'm not going.' 'Suit yerself,' replied Curl.

"Now I've heard everything," I told Truthful. "What happened after that?"

"Curly took Burly to Hayman Island. After a week, Curly sent a telegram to his wife: 'Having marvellous time but bad trot punting please wire $100.'

"The marriage didn't last, for some reason. But Curly and Burly are still the best of mates. A'course, that story happened a long time ago. But I helped Australian men wake up to their bloody selves.

"Now, Australian men, and women, are learning to treat their opposites as mates as well as lovers. You wouldn't get a better looking, more intelligent or sexy person than the average Australian woman.

"And you and me – and Curly – can guarantee that Australian men are great lovers."

# White or Wrong

People who read *People* know about my old mate the late Captain Major (Lapgnayarri). He was just one of the great characters in the Gurindji Aborigines' saga.

I travelled to Wave Hill, in the Northern Territory, to celebrate two events: the Gurindji Aboriginal strike of August 1966, and the granting of Land Rights to them by Gough Whitlam in August, 1975.

Two photographers came with me, and an ABC television crew.

A picture is worth a thousand words (they say); you're getting both pictures and words.

We left Darwin at dawn and after driving all day reached the boundary fence of the Gurindji cattle station, 400km west of Katherine, towards sundown.

I leaned on the fence. When I first travelled past here 20 years ago there was no such fence. Lord Vestey leased 7800 square kilometres on either side of where I stood; now the Gurindji held freehold on 7800 square kilometres in front of me.

Standing there I recalled "Pincher" Numiari, another Gurindji leader who died recently. He had said to me: "All we want is that Vestey mob to go away from here. All this is Gurindji country!"

Well, the Vestey mob didn't go away but they were made to hand over half the Wave Hill lease (for which, by the way, they had been paying the princely sum of 20 cents per square kilometre per year).

I looked back from the fence which divided the new Vestey cattle station from that of the Gurindji. Ahead of us lay the Wave Hill settlement and 8km beyond it the Daguaru ("place for us") cattle station.

When we reached the settlement there were only three buildings, the same as 20 years before: a house, a little school (now a shop) and the police station.

I looked into the setting sun and thought I was seeing a bloody mirage about a kilometre away. Either it was a mirage or the bureaucratic bastards of the Federal and NT Aministration had built a town nearly as big as Katherine, right in the middle of the Gurindji Cattle Station.

The town was no mirage. We stayed there overnight.

At dawn I was driven to Wattie Creek (Daguaru) by Gerry who, with Vincent Lingiari, is the only survivor among the remarkable men who led the Wave Hill strike in 1966.

On the way, Gerry mentioned three things: the building of the town had divided the people physically, some families living there and some at Wattie Creek; he had sacked a contracted white musterer and officials of three Darwin Administration departments had come down to reverse his decision; and his main complaint – the modern school had been built in the "Open Town" instead of at Wattie Creek, where Whitlam had promised it would be built when he came for the land rights ceremony in 1975.

I thought of lines from Ted Egan's song *Gurindji Blues:*
But poor bugger blackfeller this country
Gov'ment boss him talk long we
Build you house with electricity
But at Wave Hill for can't you see
Wattie Creek belong to Lord Vestey
O poor bugger me
Gurindji
Not much has changed in 20 years.

The first person I met at Wattie Creek was Amy, the widow of Captain Major. She came out of the office, wearing a colourful dress and a woollen hat. She cried, and I cried too, that Major might be and we might be "released from sorrow" in the terms of the Aboriginal burial ceremony, Pukamuni.

Next day, I met Vincent Lingiari, the charismatic man who had led the walkoff and held the people together during the 20 years of pressure and hard work, building up what is one of the most viable and successful cattle enterprises in the Northern Territory.

Vincent now is old, very ill and close to death.

We sat on the side of his bed, in the kinship area he shares with his daughters and grandchildren – and a young Aboriginal "minder".

Before I left Sydney, Professor Fred Hollows had asked me to check if Vincent could still see. Fred had twice operated on Vincent's eyes at the Prince Alfred Hospital in Sydney (the last operation had been filmed by *60 Minutes*) and had restored three quarters of normal vision in one eye. Vincent had been a victim of the diseases, widespread until the intervention of Fred Hollows 10 years ago – glaucoma and trachoma.

I held up my right hand with fingers and thumb outspread. "How many fingers, Vincent?" I asked.

"Five!" Vincent replied.

Vincent Lingiari said he wanted to hold a meeting while I was there.

I talked to most members of the tribe, individually and in groups, and was again struck by their infinite variety and rich inner life – and, of course, their marvellous sense of humour.

One day a chubby, genial old friend, Bandy, came along; on his shoulder was the wierdest looking parrot I ever saw; its feathers were the colour of the desert dust and it carried on a screeching monologue that nearly burst the eardrums.

"Where did you get that bloody parrot?" I asked Bandy. He grinned impishly and said he had found it in the bush.

I asserted that there were no parrots in the district, and Bandy replied: "That bloody parrot musta bin run away from Vesteys like we did!"

On the fourth day I arrived at Wattie Creek, to be told that Vincent Lingiari had called a meeting of himself and myself, Gerry, Donald, his son Victor and a couple of others.

He wanted me to bring the "talking box", his name for the cassette recorder; the "talking box" seems to make it official. We gathered out in the bush.

We would each speak in turn. Donald asked a strange question: "Can them white fellas move buildings?"

I said I'd seen them do it in Melbourne and Moscow.

Donald then insisted that Gough Whitlam had said, in

1975, that he would build the school house at Wattie Creek, not over at Open Town. (I checked Whitlam's speech later; Donald was on the mark – men who can't read have good memories.)

Vincent then moved, and they carried, a motion that the school should be moved to Wattie Creek.

The second most important issue was sovereignty and independence. They wanted the right to make their own decisions and their own mistakes.

Gerry had sacked the contract musterer, who had insisted on mustering again this season with the helicopter instead of horsemen, because he felt the station should muster with stockmen on horses, to give employment to the young Gurindji ringers. The contract musterer wasn't needed any more.

And they didn't need the accountant at Katherine. The books should be brought back from Katherine to Amy's office at Wattie Creek, and Donald's son and other teenage Gurindji could keep the books with guidance from an ADC accountant from Darwin.

Vincent kept stressing that they should use the same tactics as 20 years before: "A little bit at a time. Them Darwin and Canberra mob got a bag of tricks; we gottem our own bag of tricks and we turn their tricks around – a little bit at a time."

Next day, there was a meeting of the whole tribe, including the children, who were brought by their favourite teacher, Kerry.

Vincent's plan was unanimously endorsed after the tribe heard several speakers, including an electrifying address by Victor Lingiari, a chip off the old block.

Kerry said that he would start teaching a day a week at Wattie Creek immediately.

After a week, I left promising to return with Fred Hollows – and Brian Manning from Darwin, who had a scheme for the Gurindji to produce smoked meat.

At Katherine, the accountant reluctantly allowed me to inspect the books. The Gurindji had $69,000 in the bank, and owed only $27,000 – and the present muster will realise something like 1500 head of cattle.

Eat your words, White Australia!

# Hardyarn

To the Gurindji a white cattle station manager is the lowest being on earth. No doubt, that is because of the way they and other Aborigines were treated on cattle stations until recent years.

I had come to Wattie Creek without a hat. When my forehead and nose had become severely burned, Gerry had insisted that I borrow one of his 10-gallon hats . . .

Next day I was wearing the hat when Inverway Mick, who since Major's death was the number one Gurindji wit, strolled by, saying out of the corner of his mouth: "You better take that hat off, Frank, you look like a bloody station manager."

# Salt Beef and Bread

When I arrived at Wattie Creek I half-expected to hear a witty, raucous voice call out: "You white bastard! What you doin' back here? Stirrin' up trouble again for the Vestey mob?"

But, as I got out of the 4WD in the south-west Northern Territory village, I knew the voice had been stilled.

Captain Major, or to use his true Aboriginal name, Lapgnayarri, had died early this year. I called him Lapna, or Major, for short.

He had greeted me with this outrageous but friendly remark on many occasions since I first went to Wattie Creek to see the Gurindji in 1966. That year, they walked off the Wave Hill cattle station, owned by Lord Vesty himself.

I was to learn slowly that this was the first strike for Land Rights by an Aboriginal tribe.

Lapna led the first of the cattle station strikes by Aborigines in 1966, at Newcastle Waters station.

When the Gurindji tribal elder, Vincent Lingiari, led his people off Wave Hill, Major returned there with his wife Amy.

The Gurindji waited, first on the dry bank of the Victoria River, then behind the Welfare Settlement, for two years. It was the longest strike in history.

I found myself drawn into their aura of nobility and stoic courage. I visited them frequently and helped them organise a nationwide campaign in support of their claim that the Wave Hill cattle station should be returned to them by Lord Vestey because it was their tribal land.

After two years of some interest and support from sections of the white Australian community, most people wanted to forget the Gurindji. And then in 1968, the Minister for Aboriginal Affairs put before the Gorton Cabinet a proposal that the Gurindji be granted 10 square kilometres around Wattie Creek. The proposal was defeated without even going to a vote.

Meanwhile the Gurindji occupied Wattie Creek and began to build simple buildings there.

In 1970 the Federal Government withdrew their pensions and dole, and we formed a Save The Gurindji committee in Melbourne and Sydney.

In Sydney, thousands of people, black and white, gathered in front of Vestey's office in George Street; 147 people were arrested, including, I'm proud to say, yours truly.

During the struggle, which lasted until 1975 (when Gough Whitlam excised about half the Wave Hill cattle station and granted it in freehold to the Gurindji at a ceremony at Wattie Creek), Lapgnayarri was one of the leaders of the work to build up the Gurindji Cattle Station, and he visited southern cities several times, speaking on their behalf.

Lapna had never been to school and could neither read nor write, but he was a witty and fluent speaker, capable of holding his own with the best of them, whether at a factory gate, on a ship or wharf, or on a university campus. He had to be the greatest yarn spinner I ever heard: he could have played me and Tall-tale Tex Tyrrell off a break.

His story of how the Gurindji first saw cattle is a classic. He told it in the film I made in 1971 for ATV Television (London), based on my book *The Unlucky Australians*.

The tele-documentary was shown in more than 30 countries, including England, Germany, Japan and America, but never in Australia!

It remains one of the bitterest things in my life that it was not shown here.

Lapna's grandfather, Burrunjuk, was out hunting for scrub turkey when he came upon a herd of cattle drinking by Wattie Creek.

He said to them in Gurindji, "G'day." They could merely reply, "Moo!"

Burrunjuk went back to report that he had found a tribe with split hoof and horns, whose language had only one word.

Next day the whole tribe went out to have a look. An elder

spoke to one of the animals and received the same reply as Burrunjuk. Then a big bull charged the elder and seriously wounded him.

Needless to say, Burrunjuk killed the offending bull with a spear and, after a while, the Gurindji decided this was not a new tribe after all, but an edible animal. So they began to kill the occasional cow and eat it.

The white cattlemen mounted punitive attacks, killing several Gurindji people. But the Gurindji acted in self-defence.

# *Hardy*arn

When Lapgnayarri first visited Sydney, he was confronted at the airport.

A journalist asked him: "Do you mean to tell us that all the Aboriginals got to eat at Wave Hill Cattle Station was a little bit of flour, sugar and tea, and salt beef?"

Lapna gave a white, toothy grin and replied: "Oh, sometimes they bin put an extra bit of salt on the beef!"

After a silence, this crack brought the house down and Major followed up by suggesting that perhaps the proper currency for a transaction for the Gurindji to buy back their land from Lord Vestey would be salt beef and bread!

# Great Leapin' Leprechauns

Dave Allen was born David Tynan O'Mahoney in July, 1936. He's had a hard life; he's been a stand-up comedian since he was 19.

After four years kidding the Irish to laugh at themselves, he crossed the Irish Sea.

In 1959, he made his first television appearance in the London BBC program *New Faces*. I'd like to report that he became a star overnight but, in fact, he went down like a lead balloon. He commented later: "That was the longest, most terrifying three minutes of my life!"

In 1961 a certain tour of the provinces passed almost unnoticed. The band was unknown – The Beatles. The warm-up man and compere was absolutely unknown – Dave Allen.

The Beatles went on to become the greatest popular music group of our time – and I'm here to say that Dave Allen has become the greatest stage and television comedian of our time.

My own first memory of Dave Allen was of him leaping like a lunatic leprechaun on a trampoline on his Channel Nine show, *Tonight With Dave Allen*.

We first met at that time in Neptune's Restaurant, Kings Cross. He told me he'd suggested to Ken Hall, then manager of Channel Nine, that he should make *Power Without Glory* into a television series. "He didn't exactly snap the idea up," Dave said with his inimitable air of contrived innocence. "I wonder why?"

Dave was right. Ten years later *Power Without Glory* became the most successful television drama shown in Australia. The ABC not Channel Nine made it: I wonder why?

I've spent many an evening with Dave Allen – in Melbourne, Sydney and London – most recently in Sydney during his current tour of Australia.

I rang the Sebel Town House, didn't I? And left a message and Dave soon rings back, doesn't he?

"Dave Allen," he says and I say: "I hope your God still goes with you." And Dave says: "I hope so, because I'm doing a three-month tour of Australia under the management of Pat Condon. He told me you were in Melbourne. Let's get together."

"Mister," I said, quick as a flash, "Get me a free ticket at the Opera House!"

"The place is sold out," Dave tells me, "but I'll personally put an extra chair on stage for you."

An evening with Dave Allen can't be described – it has to be experienced. His jokes can't be written – you have to hear him tell them.

That night he did routines and told stories about children and parents, religion and racism, sex and society, airlines and advertising, politics and parking attendants.

The audience giggled, guffawed, winced, belly-laughed and occasionally went into collective convulsions.

At the end, Dave said with an air of seriousness, "I never give encores." He described how most performers walk off stage, wait behind a curtain for the audience to applaud, then come back several times. "I never do that. You will think it's because I'm too honest, got too much integrity. That's not the reason: I've waited behind too many bloody curtains and no one clapped."

With that he walked off. The audience clapped warmly, the stage was blacked out, and the lights came on again – and Dave Allen returned.

The applause was thunderous: "He's going to give encores after all." But Dave simply picked up half a glass of champagne he'd left on his only prop, a stool, grinned impishly and hurried off. The audience loved it and went away, still laughing and somehow thoughtful.

I realised that Dave Allen had transformed those people. They had not only been entertained, they had been educated, changed for the better in some magical way.

Speaking about the nature of humour, Dave Allen once said: "A laugh is an immediate reaction; and laugh or not, after a moment you surely can't help thinking of the reality behind the gag."

The reality behind the gag! That's Dave Allen's secret. He is a thinking person's comedian – or rather, he's a comedian who can make people laugh and think at the same time.

Over the years, critics all over the world – his TV series *Dave Allen At Large* is shown on both sides of the Iron Curtain, in more countries than the United Nations has on its books – have tried to sum up Dave's genius. To quote but a few: "A mystery of illogical logic"; "a roaming, rambling, funny and wicked onslaught on all things we are taught to believe . . ."; "a scandalous superb story teller" . . . and so on.

As a comedian, Dave Allen has got wit, style, charm, irony, and perfect timing – and above all he cares about the fate of his fellow men and women. This latter quality shows through in his writing, painting and documentary films.

In the dressing room after the show, I told Dave he was as good as ever. To which he replied: "My humour often comes from anger these days – I'm bloody furious at some things that are going on in the world."

Exchanging yarns and experiences since we last met, I recalled Dave coming to the launching of my book *Who Shot George Kirland?* in Melbourne in 1980 – and the newspaper photographs of him about to pour a pint of beer over me – and the book.

He told me about an experience he had in London with a parking attendant (for that read Grey Ghost).

One of these ogres booked Dave for parking a few minutes over the limit.

Dave did his lollie and pointed out that the said attendant had failed to book two Bentleys outside a fashionable betting shop nearby.

At last, with that marvellous anger of his, Dave drove across London to the Transport Authority's office to report the Grey Ghost.

His complaint fell on deaf ears.

And when he came out of the building he'd collected another parking ticket.

We left the Opera House – three car loads of Dave's legions of Sydney friends.

I got to the New York Deli at Double Bay before Dave, took some enveloped parking fines out of my glove box and arranged them in neat rows under the windscreen wipers.

Dave winced and inspected the car, smiling his approbation. A bystander said: "That's Dave Allen and he's collected a dozen parking fines."

After a supper washed down with wine and wondrous conversation, I drove Dave back to the Sebel Town House.

I went for a run on the rails, only to be blocked by a parked car.

"Book the bastard," says Dave. So I got out and put one of my parking tickets on the offending car.

As we passed an exclusive, illegal gambling joint in Double Bay, Dave ordered me to stop, took a couple of envelopes from the windscreen and "booked" a Bentley and Mercedes.

We both laughed all the way into town – all I had to do to get rid of my parking fines was put them on flash cars.

"The bastards might pay them," Dave said.

"They will," I answered. "They've got bigger offences on their minds than parking fines!"

# *Hardyarn*

I've heard Dave Allen tell hundreds of yarns on stage and off.

One of my favourites goes something like this:

Two Irishmen, Pat and Mick, were close friends. Pat calls to pick Mick up for their daily trip to the pub. Mick says he can't come because his father is dead.

And sure enough, there was Mick's father all dressed up for the wake, sitting next to Mick, as dead as a dodo.

So Pat says: "He's got a suit on – we'll take him with us, sit him up in a chair and put a glass in his hand. Nobody'll be any wiser."

Well, they have a few jars with the father sitting there with a glass in his hand.

Towards closing time, Pat says he's going to the "john" and Mick goes with him. A barman comes to clear up the table and take the glasses away. He says to the old man, "I hope you had a good time but you'll have to drink up now."

The barman gives Mick's father a friendly slap on the shoulder and the dead body slides off the chair and slumps on the floor.

When Pat and Mick come back, the barman says: "I wouldn't have laid a hand on him only he pulled a gun on me."

You should hear Dave Allen tell that one!

# Adieu, Signoret

News of the death of Simone Signoret came as a shock to me . . . and brought back memories of my French period in the late '70s.

In 1975 two significant events occurred which influenced my life: Kerr kicked Whitlam out; and *Power Without Glory* appeared as a television series.

The first caused me, for the first time, to actually want to get out of Australia; the second made my departure financially possible.

I chose France because a few years before I'd gone there at the invitation of actor James Mason to write a film for him and his wife, Australian actress Clarissa Kaye. Nothing came of the film but through the Masons I met Simone Signoret and her husband, Yves Montand.

They lived in a village called St Paul de Vence, so I headed back there in 1976 to write a book. On my earlier visit, I had been told the cost of living was about the same as here. And so it proved.

I went from Nice airport to La Colombe D'or hotel in St Paul, and found Simone and James Baldwin, the black American writer, sharing drinks.

"I don't believe it," Baldwin said.

Signoret (people called her simply Signoret – there was only one) said: "I thought you'd come back one day."

She smiled, a smile which in her youth would have been fetching but was now whimsical. "Well, Frank, you must admit I was a good mailbox."

This latter remark referred to when Signoret hawked my novel *But The Dead Are Many* around the offices of Paris publishers.

During my previous visit, the Masons put me up at La Colombe D'or and while there I had revised the manuscript of *But The Dead Are Many*. Signoret asked if she could read it.

Then she said to James Baldwin: "This novel is so bloody good, you're going to hate it."

Now, she reminded Jimmy of this remark and he exclaimed: "It is bloody good but I loved it."

I was suprised to see that Signoret had markedly aged and put on weight, and had a touch of gout in her right foot. Yet the beauty of her younger years remained, the fine cheekbones and lively eyes and a physical grace.

In the months ahead, during afternoon ritual drinks, I discovered that she had played few film roles since her award winning *Room At The Top*, but she was seeking scripts with suitable dramatic roles.

Meanwhile, she began writing her autobiography, which was eventually published with great success (it was the first book I read in French). Its title was brilliantly typical of Signoret's mind: *Nostalgia Is Not What It Was*. The personality of a woman of wit, political commitment and integrity shone through its pages.

When my sister Mary first showed signs of the crisis which led to her illness, she also thought of writing an autobiography. Signoret sent her an inscribed copy of *Nostalgia* encouraging Mary to persist in writing the book.

I was at La Colombe D'or the day the Israeli director came to see Signoret with an idea of making a film based on part of a book by a Palestinian Arab about the street children of Marseilles. The director wanted Signoret to play the role of a middle-aged Jewish prostitute who looks after children and befriends an Arab boy.

The result was *Madame Rosa*. The film was a triumph for Signoret and became a box-office hit throughout the world.

She loved making it because of the political and human message inherent in the story of the old Jewish prostitute playing mother to Arab youths.

When I left France in 1980, Signoret's sight was already failing and she had begun to lose weight.

When she died she was totally blind and had cancer. I remember her as a friend of infinite charm, wisdom and sensitivity to the needs of others.

Indeed, Simone, nostalgia is not what it was – but I, like millions of others, will never forget you.

# Hardyarn

Many Australian tourists have described the French as arrogantly impatient with visitors who can't speak French.

My experience contradicted this view: The French are really considerate and helpful – if you try with the language.

I arrived with scarcely a word of French, and made slow progress, mainly because most of the people I knew spoke French fluently.

I learned to read French by studying the racing form guides with the aid of a French-English dictionary. The jargon of racing writers is the same the world over. "Prefer on a dry track" (you soon discover that dry in French is 'sec'), and so on.

After a year I spoke little French and understood less, so I announced in Le Clap bar-restaurant one night that I would speak only French in future. Good natured laughter was the response, but I persevered, got a teacher and began to make progress.

My French friends made kindly remarks: "Tu parle le Francais tres bien."

"Tres mauvais," I replied. "Je parle le Francais avec un accent comme une vache Espanole (I speak French with an accent like a Spanish cow)."

Within another year, I spoke the language quite well, but my verb endings were very shaky – and my accent atrocious. Yet I decided to tell an Australian yarn in French.

I chose The Great Australian Battler yarn about Dooley Franks from Parramatta. I began to relate the adventures which ensued when Dooley went to join Tattersalls Club in Sydney.

I got laughs and was delighted: I could translate Australian idioms, and the foreigners were catching on to the Australian sense of humour!

Then I became aware of someone speaking almost simultaneously, translating the story from French to English, I thought. The punchline brought the house down.

The translating voice, that of Yves Montand, as it turned out, repeated the punchline – in French.

He had been translating the whole story from my French into French.

# The Depression You Have When You're Not . . .

Which was the worst depression – that of the '80s or that of the '30s? I was pondering the question in the Woolpack Inn, Parramatta.

Two Labor governments were arguing the toss about who was up who and who wasn't paying. Meanwhile the poorest people in NSW had their electricity cut off, went hungry or got evicted.

A reporter had asked me the question about which decade had the worst depression. I'd come down on the side of this depression being the worst.

Many people in the '80s are in debt to hire purchase companies when they become unemployed and lose fridges, cars or even houses. In the '30s, most people who lost jobs had no debts.

Then I remembered that, early in the '30s there was no dole at all; and later if a father was working, his sons couldn't get the dole – and vice versa.

If you collected rations or dole in one town, you had to move 80km before you could draw it the next week. The Government contained the anger of the unemployed by keeping them moving.

In the 1980s' depression they contain the unemployed by paying them just enough to eke out a miserable existence below the poverty line with many young people homeless.

The unemployed don't move around so much now. They become frustrated, and some turn to vandalism or drugs. And if they get heavily into drugs, they have to steal to feed their habit.

So the unemployed in the '30s were better organised and more militant than they are now. But, I am pleased to report to the people who read *People*, today's unemployed are now realising the system has failed them, and they have to organise to defend their rights and liberties.

And, first in Melbourne and now in Sydney, many of them are attracted to the Coalition Against Poverty And Unemployment, battling to have the Emergency Funding restored in NSW, for higher dole and pensions and for the right to work.

While I was thus reflecting, who should walk into the bar but Truthful Jones himeslf.

And what does he say? He says: "It's a bloody disgrace: two so-called Labor Governments playing chess with the poorest people as pawns in the game."

The bastard Jones is psychic (like the Countess of Carringbush herself) – he can read my mind. So I asked him: "Which depression was the worst?"

"Six of one and half a dozen of the other," Truthful replied, licking his lips. "But Time-Table Tommy, a famous bagman of the '30s, reckoned that the boom between depressions was bloody near as bad as the depressions themselves. I'm thirsty just thinking about it." Sensing a yarn, I bought two schooners of beer.

"Did I ever tell you about the sundowner who paid his fare out of Wagga Wagga?" Truthful Jones asked, sipping his beer.

"What's unusual about that?" I asked.

"What?! Sundowners never paid fares. It was against the rules of the Bagmen's Union. You were on the track during the Depression. You should have been a member of the Bagmen's Union. Would you believe that I wore herring tins for shoes once? And my wife, Teresa – who always liked to put on side – wore condensed milk tins for high heels?"

"This sundowner paid his fare during the depression, did he?" I ventured.

"No, just after World War II, when the boom started. The way the system works is: a depression, a war, then a boom. They talk about dole bludgers who don't want to work, yet if a war started tomorrow there'd soon be no unemployment.

"I joined the army when the war broke out. Came straight off the track. The Sixth Divvy was made up mainly of bagmen. First steady job we ever had was getting shot at.

"I joined up with Time-Table Tommy. A very cultured man, he knew the time every train left every town in four states.

"Well, me and Time-Table got discharged from the army in Queensland in 1946. Seeing as we hadn't paid a train fare since 1930, we jumped the rattler out of Brisbane by force of habit. We got to Albury easy enough, then decided to hitch-hike down the highway.

"We came on the old sundowner sitting under a peppercorn tree at Wodonga. And so help me – he's grilling a nice bit of T-bone steak on a wire griller. Corks on his hat brim, a scraggy beard, about fourpence worth of old clothes on, eyes staring like holes burned in a blanket.

"'Where did you get the flash griller, mate?' I asked him.

"'Bought it at the ironmongers in Albury,' he says.

"'That's a nice bit of steak,' Time-Table Tommy says.

"'I bought it at the butchers,' the sundowner tells him.

"Tommy says: 'Things *have* changed up on the track. Before the war, in the '30s, there were no jobs and you were lucky to get a handout of maggoty mutton.'

"Anyway, the old fella gives us a bit of steak and we hoe in. 'The track's not what it was,' he tells us, 'people keep offering you work. You get handouts of cash sometimes. And I paid me fare on a train yesterday – first time in 20 years.'

"The old sundowner told us he was up at Wagga Wagga asleep under a bridge when a farmer woke him up and said: 'Do you want a job harvesting?'

"'Not me,' he told him, 'it's against me union principles.'

"'Thirty pounds a week – and your keep,' the farmer said, 'double time for Saturdays and sleep in the house with sheets on the bed.'

"The sundowner told me and Time-Table Tommy that he had just decided to push off when up drove a Rolls-Royce and out got a flash cocky in leggings and riding breeches. 'Sorry to disturb you, old son,' he said, 'would you care for employment during the harvest? Fifty pounds a week and the use of my car at weekends.'

"The old sundowner was beginning to weaken. So he rolled his swag and legged it up the opposite bank and down to the railway station for the lick of his life. The passenger train was about to pull out. Too late to jump it. So the old sundowner had to pay his fare.

"Me and Time-Table asked him: 'And where are you going now, old-timer?'

"'To the Strzelecki ranges until after the harvest,' he told us, 'nothing grows there except gum trees and bracken.'"

"Does that story have a moral?" I asked Truthful.

"The moral is, mate," Truthful answered, "that there's either a famine or a feast. During a famine you can't find work; and during a feast, just when you've got used to not working, every bastard you meet wants to offer you a job."

# The Butchers of World War II

Australians have had a lot of influence on world events. And when they travel they learn a lot.

Two characters, Don Rountree of the Butchers' Union, in Melbourne, and Wally Wooley, a wharfie from Sydney, prove that.

Don wrote the letter that turned the tide of the war– and Wally, well, enough said.

Those people who remember World War II will know that, after Hitler attacked Russia in 1941, a great argument developed about whether Russia's Western Allies should open a second front, that is, invade Western Europe and force Hitler to fight on two fronts.

Well, Churchill, Prime Minister of England, and the Americans mucked about a fair bit, they reckon.

That's why the Butchers' Union annual meeting passed a motion for Don Rountree to write to Winston Churchill.

The full story of how the letter came to be written is published in my new book of stories *The Loser Now Will Be Later To Win*. The letter goes:

Dear Winston,

You are probably fairly busy at the moment, but I've been asked to write to you about opening that there second front in Europe.

Actually, a motion was carried at the annual general meeting of the Allied Meat Industry Employees Union (amalgamated under the Arbitration Act of 1904), at the Trades Hall, Melbourne, last Monday. The meeting was well attended (47 present).

Well, to make a long story short, this here motion was carried that you should hop in and open that there second front. We reckon it's no use you sticking to the idea that you should wait until Hitler and the Russians bleed each other to death because Hitler might beat them then invade England.

Better to get in first, or come the King Hit, as one of the speakers suggested when addressing himself to the motion at our meeting . . .

Just in case you think the attendance at the meeting was on the small side, perhaps I should mention a few names of the people present who voted with us, so you'll realise the motion was carefully worked out.

For openers, the motion itself was moved by The Fellow Slave (I'll get his real name before I send this off); he's Offal Carter at the biggest meat works in Australia owned by Sir William Angliss whom you probably know (you knighted him last New Year's Day).

And Blue Armfield seconded the motion (he won the Grand National on Reditch in 1934 but had a bad fall at Flemington and broke his neck so he got a job sweeping up the offal at the Angliss Meat Works).

And Curly Jackson was there and voted with us. Curly got the two for one for daggy and maggoty sheep at the Shepparton Abbatoirs in 1936.

So as you can see, there were some pretty smart men with their hands up when the motion was put.

I myself voted for the motion, needless to say, and I spoke about the need for a second front in Europe on the Labour Hour on Radio 3KZ, Melbourne, last Sunday. Did you hear me? When replying you might give me your opinion on how you think the broadcast went. Bluey Armfield and the boys thought I went goodo.

Well, that's about all for now, Winston, as I've got a few other letters to write. The pub over the road shuts at six o'clock – and I'm thirsty enough to drink a whisky through an Afghan camel-driver's jockstrap.

Hoping you are the same.

Yours for the second front,

Signed: D.R. Rountree, state president and federal secretary, AMIEU.

# Hardyarn

A wharfie named Wally Wooley from Woolloomooloo – they called him Woolloo for short – used to stand in the pub at Woolloomooloo with his mates of a Saturday morning, spending his last dollar on beer and saying his life's ambition was to go to Paris.

Well, one Saturday morning Woolloo's mates were standing in the pub when he rushed in and said he'd won the lottery. Shouted for the bar to prove it. Well, needless to say, his mates gave him plenty of advice.

One bloke suggested he should send his kids to the university.

"What," he answered. "And turn them into toffs and scabs? Not on your bloody life."

"Buy yourself a house," another fella urged.

"The old house I'm living in has done me for 20 years," Woolloo told him. "It's no good arguing with me. I'm going to Paris. And I'm not coming back until all the money's gone."

Within a week, he jobbed the panno, snatched his time and bought an air ticket to gay Paree.

His mates often wondered what became of Woolloo – until one lunch time, six months later. They arrived at the pub as usual and there he was, large as life, standing in the corner all dressed up to go on afternoon shift, spending his last dollar on beer.

His mates crowded around him and asked a lot of questions. "What was the weather like in Paris?" one asked.

"Not like here in Woolloomooloo. It was beautiful. I was there in the spring and summer and the sun shining every day. Not like here in Woolloomooloo where it's either too hot or too cold, either raining cats and dogs or a drought. Not like here in Woolloomooloo, I can tell you."

"And what was the tucker like in Paris?" another fellow queried.

"The tucker was beautiful," Woolloo told them. "Not like here in Woolloomooloo. You can sit on the footpath and have your meals and watch the crowds go by.

"And the food? Delicious! Turtle soup, steak, and frog's legs done in beautiful sauce. They use seasoning in the sauce that would make the sole of a leper's boot taste like a filet mignon. Boy, that was tucker. Not like the pies and sausages you get here in Woolloomooloo."

Well, they kept asking Woolloo about Paris. "Did you go to one of them there night clubs?" another mate asked.

"I went to the Folies Bergere every night, not like these crummy floor shows here in Woolloomooloo, I can tell you. It was terrific. Music. Champagne. Floor show. Dancing girls. Not like here in Woolloomooloo."

Another bloke says to him: "And what were those French women like?"

"Ah, not like these bags here in Woolloomooloo. French women are glorious – not too fat, not too thin, not too tall, not too short. Beautiful clothes and perfect figures. An old French madame is better looking than a teenage model here in Woolloomooloo."

Someone asked: "Listen, Woolloo, did you ever go to bed with a French woman?"

"My bloody oath, I did," he replied.

"And what was it like?"

Well, that rocked him a bit. He looked this way and that, drained his last beer and said: "Oh, just like here in Woolloomooloo, come to think of it. Just like here in Woolloomooloo."

# TV . . . We've Ad It!

There has been a steep fall in the number of people watching television in Australia. One of the reasons is the excessive advertising.

One recent Saturday evening, I visited singer Helen Montgomery, and her friend, Jane, to watch a couple of Bogart movies. I noticed that Helen turned the sound down every time the ads came on.

I reacted with anxiety (I've been brainwashed into needing the film interrupted every 10 minutes with about five ads). So I got Helen to leave the sound on and we studied the ads.

We learned that Joyce Mayne had a mount in the Melbourne Cup and that the song Cabaret was written only after the composer was offered a chocolate by a beautiful bird.

People used to get hooked on these ads and even went around singing the commercial jingles. Imagine it: "And now I'm wearing no knickers, I'm as happy as I can be!"

But now even kids find most ads ridiculous.

The ultimate hypocrisy was the one with the $10 note and a voice says: "Which bank has the highest credit rating in the world?" And strike me dead if I tell a lie, Henry Lawson's face on the note moves and he says: "The Commonwealth Bank."

Now, having researched Henry Lawson's life for 30 years, I can positively assert that he never had a bank account in his life – for the very good reason that he never had any money to put in one.

Then they actually put on an advertisement defending advertisements.

There is this family, see, and there they are sitting watching TV when a voice says: "In some countries they don't have advertising!"

Two blokes walk in the door and take the television set

away. Then the voice says that these poor bastards don't have freedom of choice and these two blokes take the furniture away.

Eventually, the family is left standing in an empty room.

The warning voice says: "You'd notice the advertisements more if they weren't there."

Imagine it, those "people in some countries" couldn't find their way to a furniture shop unless they saw an ad on TV.

In France ads are *not* permitted in the middle of a program, only at the beginning and the end.

That policy should be adopted in Australia. Magazines and newspapers don't put ads in the middle of articles and stories.

And magazine and newspaper advertising is much more socially useful. They advertise jobs for the jobless, sales for shoppers, birth notices and other such things that people need.

So my advice to advertisers is: spend more of their money in newspapers and magazines (especially *People* which is read by the most intelligent section of the community) and less on television.

# *Hardyarn*

I was out prospecting when I learned the real power of advertising.

Me and Truthful Jones went prospecting north of Kalgoorlie. In the desert, more than 100km from the nearest railhead.

We worked like slaves to sink a deep shaft, thinking we were on a quartz reef, but struck solid rock.

Truthful got jack of it after that, so when the truck came with mail and the weekly supplies of grub and water he took a lift back and left me there.

Well, I kept digging away. It's slow work on your own, and very lonely, especially at night. I used to lie awake listening to the dingoes howling.

Then one night I saw a light in the distance. It seemed to be fairly close by, so I headed towards it. I must have walked 5km or so – a single light always seems closer than it really is in the bush at night. There was a crescent moon casting weird shadows . . .

Eventually I came near the light. It was a carbide lamp in a lean-to made of logs and bark. There was an old codger sitting on a small box beside a big box with the lamp on it, shuffling a pack of cards. So I thinks: a poker school. The mateship of a game of cards was just what I needed.

I was just going to speak when the old fella dealt himself about 12 cards. He fanned them out in his hand, looked at them, and turned them face down on the box. Then he screwed up his face and reeled off the cards in a high-pitched cackling voice: "Ten of hearts, jack of diamonds, seven of clubs, ace of spades, six of hearts . . . "

Long white hair, moustache and beard. Bony hands like a skeleton's, covered with withered yellow leather. Bare, dirty feet. Holes in the knees of his old dungarees and a flannel singlet gone hard with sweat and dust. On his Pat Malone, see, talking to himself, as mad as a Shepparton snake.

He had an old clock there. So he wound it up and put it on the box. Then he stepped back to the entrance and listened.

He backed away from the clock towards me with his hand to his ear, listening.

Before I could get away, he bumped into me, see, and swung around – one of those mad hermits who hang around old goldfields until they die.

"What's your name?" he asked me, as if it was natural for someone to stumble into his camp in the middle of the night.

I told him and he dashed into the hut, grabbed the lamp, and held it in front of my face. "Eyes blue. Complexion dark. Height five foot eleven (178cm). I'll remember you if we meet again."

What was the purpose of him repeating the denomination of the cards, listening to the clock, and committing my name and description to memory? you may ask.

Well, it turned out that he'd seen an advertisement in an old newspaper that had come out to his camp wrapped around some groceries. He cut out a coupon and took one of them courses in Pelmanism that used to be advertised.

155

You know: "Train the mind, memory – and personality. Strengthen your will. Improve your memory and hearing. Increase your powers of concentration. Become a business executive."

I couldn't help thinking: what use would it be to him?

There he was, more than 100km from the nearest human habitation, 75 years old, and as mad as a hatter. What would he want with Pelmanism?

It shows the power of advertising, or the hunger for knowledge – I've never been able to decide which.

# Truthful Has a Few

"Where are you off to?" Truthful Jones asked me. "To Harold Park."

"Don't tell me you're hooked on the red-hots again. I thought you more a gallops man."

I assured Truthful I wasn't going to the red-hots (or even the harness racing). "My book is being launched at the Harold Park Hotel, opposite the trotting track."

Writers In The Park, they call it: every Tuesday night writers read from their works and more people turn up than to a rock band. And the Harold Park Hotel, corner Wigam Road and Ross Street, Sydney, has as good a variety of beer as you'd find in a long pub crawl.

Two dedicated people organise these readings – Kim O'Brien and George Papaellinas. And Mark Morgan, the publican, is an enthusiastic patron.

Donald Horne agreed to launch the book and – the better the day the better the deed – on November 11, the anniversary of the Kerr Coup. Donald and I had organised People For Democracy in response to the coup back in 1975-76.

Donald, with his usual touch of learned levity, praised the book, which is called *The Loser Now Will Be Later To Win,* and spoke of the threads running through the book: the Truthful Jones-Billy Borker thread of Australian humour; the *Power Without Glory* thread of social criticsm; the *But The Dead Are Many* thread of literary-psychological analysis.

He then spoke of some boozy lunches we'd had together: one when we discussed my book *The Unlucky Australians.*

He made a crack which might have been lost on some people: "Some of these lunches were paid for by the CIA."

That I had better explain!

When we first met back in the '60s Donald was, I think, editor of *Quadrant* which later was alleged to be secretly financed by the CIA.

I took Donald to task about this and he responded: "I've already quit and you needn't gloat – at least one of our lunches was paid for by the CIA without us knowing it."

Donald concluded his excellent warm-up speech by saying that I was, as well as a successful writer, a successful agitator (in the best sense of the word).

Unlike your usual book launch this one was, in the best tradition of Writers In The Park, about reading aloud – and selling books.

I had planned with the organisers and singer Helen Montgomery to read the first story in the book – with musical interludes.

The story was called *And I Must Have 50 Pounds*. The people who read *People* know the guts of the story; the swindle that Henry Lawson and Victor Daley pulled on Archibald, editor of the Sydney Bulletin. They pretended Lawson was dead and borrowed 50 quid for his funeral.

The story also takes up a couple of scenes in my play about Henry Lawson, *Who Was Harry Larsen?* Helen Montgomery had played Mary Gilmore and she sang some of the Lawson poems set to music by Chris Kempster. The other songs were originally sung by the late Declan Affley.

At appropriate moments Helen sang *Keep Step 103* and *Do You Think That I Do Not Know.* The audience loved her, notwithstanding that she broke down in the middle of the second verse of the love song.

She told me afterwards that she can't get through those songs anymore without crying from the sheer sadness of Declan dying.

Declan Affley of course couldn't be present (Truthful Jones reckons that Lucifer has put a strict curfew on him) so we played from a cassette of Declan singing *Faces In The Street, The Old Rebel Flag In The Rear* and *Freedom On The Wallaby.*

These were moments of haunting magic.

The performance lasted bloody near an hour and it was red-hot in that lounge bar. But the audience had been caught up in the spirit of Lawson and Daley and the other great revoluntionary bohemians of the 1890s.

At the interval I got writer's cramp autographing books.

Not only was the lounge bar packed to the gunwales but amongst the crowd were some very distinguished people: Myfanwy Gollan (Horne), Margaret Jones from *The Sydney Morning Herald* no less, Rosa Franykl Luxembourg, Harry Reade from Cuba, Nicholas and Julia Horne.

Truthful Jones came, although admittedly he turned up late and pissed out of his mind.

So get yourself along to the Harold Park Hotel any Tuesday at 8pm. A good time guaranteed!

# *Hardyarn*

For an encore at the Harold Park pub that night, I read another story from *The Loser Now Will Be Later To Win* called *Christmas Comes But Once.*

There's this bloke who's been unemployed for years and has got used to it when he falls in love with a beautiful bird and decides to do two very foolish things: to get a job and get married.

I don't have to tell you how difficult it is for a person who's been on the dole to get a job. It's bloody near impossible.

But this bloke, Harvey Johnson by name, ends up getting a job as Father Christmas. And he has to ride an elephant up Smith Street, Carringbush.

Along the way, he discovers that the elephant's attendant, Black Alan, likes his drop of beer and goes into every pub leaving Harvey sitting on the elephant, named Matilda, in a temperature of 40 degrees with more clothes on than an Arctic explorer.

Fair enough! But it turns out that Matilda is a bigger toss pot than her attendant, so she slaps her trunk on the wall of the pub, until Black Alan comes out with a silver tray of beer and Condy's crystals.

Matilda slurped this down so the publican brings out a bucket of beer.

Eventually Harvey Johnson himself gets on the booze.

At last they move off up Smith Street, Father Christmas on a drunk elephant with a drunk attendant loping along beside.

To make a long story short, Father Christmas eventually arrives at the department store on the elephant. He'd adjusted his beard and was ho-hoing away when Matilda went beserk and proceeded to wreck the joint.

You will really have to buy the book or borrow it from a library to get the full flavour of this yarn.

Suffice to say here, Harvey lost his job as Father Christmas; his girlfriend gave him the old heave-ho; and he went back on the dole.

# Here's to Hughie

Preparing for this story I went around bookshops seeking a book on toasts. One lady bookseller told me: "We've got do-it-yourself books on every subject on earth – except making toast."

"Moving toasts," says I.

The best I could find was a book called *Wedding Etiquette*. From it, I found out some extraordinary trivia, for example the Royal toast: "Formally, there should be no smoking before this toast."

"Over the years all over the world I've heard toasts moved: pompous toasts; funny toasts; and outrageous toasts.

And the funniest, most incongruous and outrageous toast I ever heard moved was at a state luncheon in East Berlin (of all places). The occasion was a meeting of writers from all over the world to celebrate the 25th anniversary of the defeat of Adolf Hitler's armies.

Delegates came from many countries, East and West. Among them were many notable men; the late Pablo Neruda, Louis Aragon, Constantine Siminov, et al.

The largest delegation of course was the Russians. And the second was the Australians. This was due to the fact that the air tickets were free. (I never did meet an Australian who could resist a free air ticket to anywhere).

From memory, the Australian delegation included John Morrison, Clem Christesen, Bill Wannan, Max Harris, Geoffrey Dutton and many others. The main celebrations were held in the historic city of Dresden, which had been wiped out in a horrifying and unnecessary air attack and been restored with German thoroughness – and we had a ball.

161

On the way back from Dresden, the East German government gave a state dinner to which two members of each delegation were invited. For reasons best known to themselves, the Australian delegates elected me and Max Harris (perhaps because we represented the Left and the Right).

Being patriotic Australians, we decided to arrive very early. So early, that we were first there and stood waiting in the foyer.

German officials and others arriving mistook us for the welcoming committee and shook our hands. Nothing loathe, we shook hands and bowed gracefully until the actual welcoming committee arrived.

Now, to get the full impact of the outrageous climax of this story, I have to introduce to you the central character, an old mate of mine, the late Hugh MacDiarmid.

Hughie was the greatest Scottish poet since Robert Burns and one of the great characters of our time. A fanatical Scottish nationalist, he had refused to be part of the English delegation and came as the lone Scotsman.

Hugh MacDiarmid was at that time (1968) well into his 70s. I shared a room with him and we went on the town every night. The old bastard wouldn't go to bed until at least four in the morning and drank scotch whisky as if it was going out of fashion. He excused this excess by saying he couldn't afford to drink much of it in Scotland.

When he arrived at the luncheon, looking distinguished with his white hair and moustache, but to my practised eye, as pissed as an owl, I took him by the arm and sat him down next to me.

Soon all were seated and proceedings began with German efficiency.

The main toast, to the 25th anniversary of the defeat of Fascism, was moved by a German in military uniform.

He made an excellent speech but it was long and doubled in length because it was being translated into several languages. Those were the days before pre-recorded translations through headphones so interpreters were dotted around the enormous table whispering the translation into the ears of the assembled h'authors.

Trouble was, Hughie downed three glasses of neat scotch, then went to sleep. I didn't try to wake him knowing that to be the safest condition for this wonderful, outrageous character to be in.

The speech covered the whole history of Hitler Fascism, stressing the resistance of Germans to Hitler and the horror of the concentration camps. I remember him quoting the infamous Ilse Koch: he reminded his earnest listeners that this terrible woman had made banjo covers out of skin peeled from the posteriors of concentration camp victims.

Now, it must be understood that Hugh MacDiarmid had five outstanding qualities: his greatness as a poet, his unparalleled ability to drink whisky, his contempt for English royalty, his eccentric capacity to do the opposite to everyone else (he wrote a letter to *The Times* in 1956 announcing that he had joined the British Communist Party simply because all the backward Pommy intellectuals were leaving it) – and a sense of humour so subtle that you were sometimes uncertain if he was really joking.

When the toast speech was over, the chairman, to my horror, announced that he had decided that the response to the toast should be given by none other than Hughie himself. The man explained that, although there were two Stalin prize-winners and one Nobel prize-winner present, everyone would surely agree that MacDiarmid, in his opinion the greatest writer of poetry in English and the eldest statesman of the luncheon, was the most appropriate choice.

My problem was to wake Hughie up. This I achieved only by shaking him vigorously and slapping his face.

"Hugie," I whispered.

"You've got to respond to the toast!"

"What! What! What!" Hughie replied.

I whispered right into his ear, even making a couple of suggestions of what he might say, in belief that he had heard hardly a word of the speech.

I bargained without the fact that Hughie had another outstanding characteristic: when flaked out with booze, he somehow managed to pick up a sentence or two of what was being said around him.

He rose unsteadily to his full height – he was a magnificent looking man – and reached for the nearest bottle of scotch, and an enormous mineral water glass, which he filled with his sacred national drink.

Hughie raised his glass, high towards heaven – everyone waited with bated breath to hear the response of the great Scottish poet.

"Kamarads!!" Hughie said with a lilting Scottish voice and an expression of earnest love. "May the skins of your arses never again be used for makin' banjo covers!"

# The Biggest Pumpkin Ever Grew

There I am, still hanging around the Carringbush Hotel, Collingwood, when Truthful Jones walks in again – wearing a new sports jacket and grey trousers.

"Must have been running some chook raffles by the look of you," says I, buying the drinks.

Truthful takes a big sip and says: "The crookest raffle ever run in Melbourne was run in Preston by a fella called Trigger MacIntosh. Don't know how he got that nickname but I know he had 13 kids. He raffled a pumpkin."

"But people wouldn't buy a ticket in a raffle for a pumpkin, surely," I comments.

"Australians will buy raffle tickets in anything. Anyway, this was the biggest pumpkin ever grown in the history of the world. It was so big it took six men six hours to dig it out of the ground."

"But pumpkins don't grow under the ground . . ."

"This one was so heavy it sunk into the ground 'till you couldn't see it. It took six men six hours to dig it out, and the same six men another six hours to roll it up six planks onto a six-tonne truck.

"Actually, Trigger MacIntosh owned this pumpkin in partnership with another fella, name of Greenfingers Stratton. Old Greenfingers could grow a crop of show orchids on a concrete footpath.

"Well, they decided to grow pumpkins on the river bank; very rich soil. Greenfingers went to work and pretty soon pumpkin vines began to crawl across the creek, over some paddocks of lucerne and up the side of a cocky's house.

"Anyhow, Trigger and Greenfingers waited for the pumpkins to grow but nothing happened until one day one solitary pumpkin began to grow right in the middle of the paddock.

"It grew so fast you could see it bulging. It became so

heavy it began to sink into the ground. And eventually it took six men . . ."

I says: "Yes, I know, six men six hours to dig it out. Have another drink and come to the point."

"They made a lot of money raffling it. It wouldn't fit in the pub door, so they left it on the truck outside. And Trigger put a sign on it: The Biggest Pumpkin Ever Grew – Sixpence A Ticket. Bought six raffle books at the newsagent's with 100 tickets in each . . ."

"Did they sell all the tickets?"

"For sure – in the Royal Hotel. Just before closing time, the raffle was drawn."

"Who won it?"

"Old Greenfingers himself, naturally. Eventually they raffled the pumpkin six times."

And, I said, "I suppose this bloke Greenfingers won it every time? One of these days someone is going to kill you right in the middle of one of your stories."

"Greenfingers Stratton won the first raffle on account of Trigger MacIntosh had a ticket with a secret mark on it. Anyway, the next Saturday they brought the pumpkin back to the pub again."

"Be a bit awkward wouldn't it? Raffling the biggest pumpkin ever grew more than once."

"Matter of fact, they changed the sign to read The Second Biggest Pumpkin Ever Grew and sold 600 tickets again and Old Greenfingers won it. They raffled on until they arrived one Saturday morning with the sixth biggest pumpkin ever grew . . ."

"Needless to say, that pumpkin was becoming a bit the worse for wear, what with people climbing up on it to drink their beer. It was bruised and battered. Now, for some reason certain people, wowsers and the like, started to say the raffles weren't fair dinkum.

"Anyhow, Danny O'Connell, the publican, said to Trigger: 'Listen, that there sixth biggest pumpkin that ever grew. I seem to have seen it somewhere before.' Trigger said: 'A simple case of mistaken identity.'

"O'Connell didn't like raffles being run in his pub on account he preferred his customers to spend their money on beer and bets with the SP bookie who O'Connell financed, see.

"So he says to Trigger: 'Some of my customers are complaining. They say Greenfingers Stratton won your raffle five weeks in a row.' Trigger had a good answer as usual. He said: 'Old Greenfingers was always lucky.' 'Yeh,' O'Connell replied, 'and he's working with a very lucky partner, too.'"

"Anyway, in spite of some publicity, they'd sold three books of tickets. Then Danny O'Connell says: 'Just a minute, I'll draw the raffle this week.'"

"Well, you can imagine how Trigger felt. He loses all his capital if someone wins that pumpkin off him. So he's thinkin' fast. 'You can draw it at five to six,' he tells O'Connell. Then he calls Greenfingers aside and says: 'Here's some raffle books. Go and lock yourself in the dunny and fill out tickets in my name'."

"So old Trigger won the sixth raffle himself?"

"As a matter of fact, a bloke named Sniffy Connors won the raffle with the only ticket he ever bought in his life. Trigger had only half the tickets but O'Connell drew out the one Sniffy bought."

"And what did Sniffy do with the pumpkin? Eat it?"

"Sniffy was living in a tent at the time, so he blew a hole in the side of the pumpkin with a stick of gelignite and made a house out of it. Lived in it for six years with his wife and six kids . . . "

"You win. Have another beer."

"Not me. I'm too busy today. Running a raffle. The biggest turkey ever bred in Australia. Thirty cents a time. How many tickets do you want?"

# *Hardy*arn

The raffle king of Footscray, Raffles Rogers, arrived at the Ashley Hotel to raffle a spin dryer. It fell off a truck, he explained to his regular clients.

Some Smart Alec said: "What if the bloody thing doesn't work?"

Nothing loathe, Raffles sold two books of tickets, put them in the dryer and plugged it in. It worked all right and the raffle was more fair dinkum than a lot of government-run ones.

# It's All So Taxing

Robin Hood, of Sherwood Forest, used to rob the rich and give it to the poor.

In his tax plan White Paper, Robbing Hood Keating proposes to rob the poor and give it to the rich.

Be on your guard, dear people who read *People*.

Start with the 12.5 per cent across-the-board consumption tax. A whole new range of goods and services will be caught in this net – services essential to the poorest section of the community: food, clothing, rent, public transport.

Sales tax will be cancelled and replaced by this 12.5 per cent consumption tax. Sales tax, at the moment, varies from 7.5 per cent on essential items (which will now rise by 5 per cent) and up to 32.5 per cent for luxury goods. For example, tax on luxury goods like expensive jewellery, furs, cameras, stereos and video recorders will drop by 20 per cent.

Hands up those on average or low wages or social services who buy expensive jewellery, furs and the like!

Take a gander at another aspect: as people earn more, their consumption falls according to their income. After all there is a limit to what the Double Bay and Toorak push can eat and drink.

Make no mistake, this consumption tax will cause the rich to become richer and the poor to become poorer.

Keating and Hawke are talking about compensating the poor by increasing social services but there is no way in the wide world that these increases will pull up the slack.

The most sinister part of the package is the plan to introduce identity cards. What earthly use can an identity card be in a free society?

I'm here to tell yer that the only reason is to stop dole recipients and women on single mothers' pensions from having a part-time job on the side! This is the only "fiddle" open to the poor. No one can exist, let alone live, on the dole or pension.

So, for example, a woman bringing up a child or children

on the pension will be effectively prevented from taking a few hours' casual work here and there to prevent her children from starving.

The perks of highly paid people, politicans and multi-national companies will be little affected. The capital gains tax will, of course, prevent small fry (family companies and the like) from tax dodging but the really wealthy companies will escape scot-free.

For example, both Westpac and BHP showed a profit last financial year of nearly $300 million. Will that profit be taxed at the rate of 40 per cent or 50 per cent? Not on your sweet Nellie! That profit is after tax (they are allowed to use the trick of setting money aside for paying tax). The contribution of Company Tax to overall Commonwealth revenue has fallen by 40 per cent.

This country is largely run on the basis of pay-as-you-earn tax: the only people who genuinely pay their taxes are wage and salary earners who have it taken out of their wages every week.

Make no mistake about it, this new tax program discriminates against the poor, the wage and salary earner, the farmer and the small businessman.

Why didn't this Labor Government introduce wealth tax on multi-millionaires and multinational companies, making tens of millions in profit each year? The reason they give is that if they tax the wealthy, they'll stop investing and there will be fewer jobs.

We hear a lot about strikes of labour but nothing about strikes of capital. One of the strangest developments in this country in recent years is that the majority of people seem to blame strikes of labour, while the wealthy capitalists refuse to invest unless they can make super profits.

The politicians and economists excuse this by saying that if the multinationals make huge profits, some will filter down in the form of increased employment and wages for employees.

There is only one word to describe this: Bullshit!

The fact is that the economic system proceeds in series of booms and busts. The big bust is here and the poor are going to pay.

# *Hardyarn*

"To the haves shall be given and the have-nots shall be touched for their last dollar," Truthful Jones misquoted the Bible in the Carringbush Hotel. "Anyway, money doesn't make much difference."

"You could have fooled me," I replied, buying another drink.

"A feller named Sheckles Mitchell was always trying to make money. He tried everything: selling gum leaves, hotdogs, home-made pickles, insurance policies, vacuum cleaners, encyclopedias and second-hand cars. He tried SP betting, interstate truck driving and chicken sexing. But he couldn't get in front.

"Then he invented a trouser hanger and began to manufacture them in a shed in his backyard. He put them on the market and they sold like hot cakes. Anyway, pretty soon he had a factory and 10 women working for him. That's the secret, mate, get other people working for you."

Anyway, Truthful continued, "One day he comes home and says to his missus: 'Now, darling, I've got money. Is there anyting you want?' 'Well,' his missus says, 'there is one thing. Everyone in the street has a barbecue in their backyard.' 'Say no more,' he tells her, 'get one put in right away – the best in the street.' So they get the barbecue put in.

"Well, next June he comes home and tells his wife: 'Just say the word darling, if there's anything you want.' 'Well, there is just one more thing: having the didee in the backyard isn't very convenient.' 'How right you are,' he says, 'get the plumbers in and build the best toilet money can buy, right inside the house. Spare no expense.'"

"A man who spent his money wisely," I said.

"You can say that again," Truthful replied. "Trouble was, he used to get on his mates' nerves down at the club – always bashing their ear about how much money he was making.

"One of his mates says to Sheckles: 'Listen, Sheckles, you are always yak-yaking about how much money you're making. What difference has all the money made?'"

"Well, the old Sheckles thinks for a minute, looks a bit puzzled and the says: 'Before I had money, I used to eat in the house and go to the toilet in the backyard. Now I eat in the backyard and go to the toilet in the house!'"

# The Mate Debate

Have you ever had one of those days that starts too early and too badly for any good to come of it?

Last month I had a beauty. It began at six am when the buzzer on my safe house woke me up and the man downstairs said he was from such and such a courier service with a parcel – and it ended with a horrendous debate on the nature of mateship. The courier arrived at my door a shade on the niggly side, asked for $6 and turned real nasty when I handed him a $20 bill. "I can't change that!"

I grabbed the parcel out of his hand and a shouting match ensued through the closed door. Finally, he said he would take a cheque and departed saying: "Have a nice day."

Now, there's only one thing I dislike more than people who tell you to have a nice day and that's people who say: "I wouldn't have a clue." The term actually means: "I don't know and, even if I did, I wouldn't tell a mug like you." There are a hell of a lot of people around now who will tell you to have a nice day even after they've said "I haven't got a clue."

Having got rid of the cheerful courier, bugger me if the phone doesn't ring and a character named Ian MacNamara, producer of the ABC's Sydney radio show City Extra asks me if I care to comment on Neville Wran's statement on mateship. (Ian's got a lot of clues and he never tells you to have a nice day). So muggins dashes downstairs and buys all of the papers – Nifty himself is on the front pages declaring that mateship is dead because not enough people hated the striking train drivers.

So I thinks to meself, Nifty ought to know about mateship because he's got some great mates. Lionel Murphy's little mate is a mate of his and the little mate is a mate of Abe Saffron and Nifty of course is also a mate of Kerry Packer.

Words have lost their meaning in this country.

Needless to say, by the time Ian rang back to put me on air, I was in a mood to make sure that no right winger in Sydney would have a nice day. And I completely forgot Bernard Shaw's dictum: "If you intend to commit sedition you should do so in a manner which will make those who would otherwise want to hang you think you are joking."

My habitual sense of humour had fled and I zapped Neville and his mates and the multinationals then chucked in a few quotes from Henry Lawson himself, the apostle of mateship, asserting that mateship was part of the solidarity of working men.

I quoted a Lawson poem, *The Old Unionist:*

I don't know if the cause be wrong
Or if the cause be right —
I've had my day and sung my song,
And fought the bitter fight.
In truth, at times I can't tell what
The men are driving at,
But I've been Union thirty years and I'm too old to rat!

I also said that Lawson was fond of quoting William Lane's concept that "socialism is mateship" and that mateship was the creed of the Australian battler through the convict period, the gold diggings, the great strikes in the '90s and amongst the rank and file Anzacs, the majority of whom were, in both wars, unionists.

In the middle of the interview, I heard a click, just when I began to list Neville Wran's mates and I said to the lady announcer: "You cut me off the bloody air!"

"I'm sorry," she replied. And I said: "You're not sorry, it was done deliberately."

I hung up, went back to bed and pulled the covers over me head – satisified that I had settled the mateship issue once and for all.

But little did I know! The ABC switchboard was lit up by hundreds of callers and Ian MacNamara decided to let some of them have their say. The most hostile ones had grabbed their phones first – St Ives-Double Bay types who apparently hated all strikers. One of them suggested that he would pay for an air ticket for me to go and live in Russia;

another proposed I should go back to France, yet another said that, when they pressed the button they should have cut me off the air for good and some other democrat demanded that the ABC should never allow me on the air again.

After half an hour the callers who supported me began to come on.

Meanwhile, in the ABC studios in William Street, sat no less a person than the Leader of the Opposition, Nick Greiner, annoyed and frustrated, because he was supposed to go on air at nine o'clock instead of the mad argument about mateship. When he eventually got to the microphone he supported Neville Wran (there's a moral there somewhere).

Several newspapers also supported Nifty. Granny Herald herself went so far as to publish an editorial on the matter which ended: "Mr Wran is right. There is no anger about strikes. Australians are apathetic – or they're on strike."

Now I've been a regular reader of the Sydney Morning Herald for 30 years and, in all that time, the Herald has supported only one strike – and that strike was in Poland.

When Neville Wran and the Herald editorial writer agreed that Australians "never really get angry" about strikes it obviously didn't occur to them that the majority of Australians are trade unionists and, in a democratic country where the right to strike is guaranteed, many of them are inclined to admire the strikers for "having a go."

Hundreds of thousands of Australians have been thrown on to the scrap heap in recent years and the railway men like the miners in Wollongong earlier were fighting to prevent this happening to them.

Granny Herald carried another, more intelligent, comment. Alan Peterson reported that he heard the controversy while driving to work. "How these subjects start or finish is always a mystery because the talk is well-launched when you turn on and still going when you park, but there was much talk about mateship and how it fits into the philosophy of strikes."

He then traced the history of the word "mate" back to its origins in England and concluded: Perhaps it (mateship) is one word which Australia enriched.

Even that Bible basher Dean Shilton got into the anti-mateship act. For myself, I'll continue to abide by my father's statement: "There is no such thing as a good war or a bad strike!"

# *Hardyarn*

The most brilliant of all Henry Lawson's stories about mateship was called Macquarie's Mate.

In an outback pub, the drinkers were giving heaps to a fella named Macquarie: he was a thief, a wife starver, a cattle duffer, a pisspot, a liar and a cheat. You name any sin in the book and Macquarie had committed it, according to these blokes.

Suddenly, a shabby drunk who'd been lying on the floor of the bar listening to this diatribe against Macquarie rose to his feet and said: "Macquarie is my mate – and one thing he never did in his life: he never ran a man down behind his back."

# How Hungry Hanrahan the Cabbie Took a Cockie for a Ride

I was invited to speak at the Annual Australia Day taxi drivers' dinner at Newcastle, so I needed good yarns about taxi drivers.

I hung about Truthful Jone's haunts and eventually found him at the Harold Park Hotel.

"G'day, Truthful," I said, and explained my situation. "So I need some good taxi yarns."

"Funny you should ask about taxi stories: I'm driving a Sandy MacNab again meself, at the moment. Had a bad trot at the races. So I renewed me old cab licence."

I said: "Couldn't have done it at a better time."

"Did I ever tell you about the taxi driver who sat on the Central Station rank, Sydney, for three days and nights during the Depression?"

"No, I don't think you did. Have a drink and tell me about him," I said, asking Mark for beers.

"Don't mind if I do. Well, things were real bad in the cab game in those days. People used to hide behind a telephone post when they hailed a cab."

"What was the purpose of doing that?" I asked.

"Well, cabs would come up on the footpath after you. If you don't believe me, you can ask old Hungry Hanrahan. He's been driving Sandy McNabs for 55 years, so he ought to know.

"The greatest potsitter, multiple loader and fare fleecer that ever sat behind a steering wheel is old Hungry. It was he who sat on the Central rank for three days and nights.

"In those days the line of cabs on the rank extended into Elizabeth St, down Hunter St to Castlereagh St, then down the hill to Circular Quay.

"There was a telephone at the front of the rank and sometimes a shrewdie on the rear of the queue would ring up and send the front cab off on a wild goose chase.

"And if you left your cab to have a feed or a sleep, other drivers would shift it out of the queue to the other side of the road.

"So this bloke I'm telling you about, Hungry Hanrahan, took no risks: he slept in the cab and his wife brought him sandwiches and tea at mealtime – not a bad drop of beer this – well, at last he got to the front of the queue.

"And eventually, a big fella came out of the station. A squatter from the bush by the look of him; wide-brimmed hat, old-fashioned clothes, and kept looking around at the tall buildings.

"Needless to say, Hungry couldn't get his claws on the squatter's luggage quick enough.

"'The Australia Hotel,' the man from the back o' Bourke said after he got in the back seat.

"You wouldn't read about it, would you, waiting three days and nights then getting a fare to the Australia Hotel, about 800 metres away.

"He turned to this bloke in the back – looking around with his mouth open and his eyes sticking out so you could have knocked them off with a stick – and asked him: 'New to Sydney are you, mate?'

"'Yes,' replied the squatter, 'first time I've been down. It's a big place, isn't it? I've been recommended to the Australia Hotel.' 'And that's where I'll take you,' Hungry Hanrahan said.

"Hungry put the flag down and drove down Parramatta Road.

"Anyway, he took the squatter all the way to Parramatta, then across country to Ryde, through Pymble and along the Pacific Highway back to Sydney.

"The meter was showing 20 quid when they eventually pulled up outside the Australia Hotel."

"And did the squatter pay up?"

"The squatter said: 'I don't doubt the Australia is a good hotel, but it's too far out of the city. I'd have to do too much travelling. Could you recommend me to a good hotel in the heart of the city?'

"So Hungry drove the squatter back along the Pacific Highway through Pymble and Ryde to Parramatta, then along Parramatta Road to Sydney – and he dropped him at the Carlton Hotel opposite the Australia.

"Forty quid – the biggest taxi fare ever paid in Australia until that Yank took a cab to Mt Isa."

"You're a bigger liar than Tom Pepper," I said. "But it's a great story for me to use at the Newcastle dinner."

"If you don't believe me you can ask old Hungry Hanrahan. Still driving cabs at 80.

"No pensions for cab drivers, you know, and no sick or holiday pay.

"They just drive until they drop dead at the wheel. Did I ever tell you about the time old Hungry took a bloke to the Menangle trots and got lost?"

"No, I don't think you did, but I must go now. I'm late for an important appointment at the Carlton."

"I'm your man. My cab's parked outside – I'm driving a shift for Hungry Hanrahan. Hop in. By the way, how well do you know Sydney?"

# When It Comes to Votes, Joh Gets Peanuts

There's a bone in my throat about Joh Bjelke-Petersen and the state of Qld.

People in the south – often themselves as right-wing as Sir Joh – find it convenient to make jokes about Qld, as if every banana-bender voted for Joh and supported him in all things.

The Bjelke-Petersen government gets the votes of less than 40 per cent of the Qld electorate. Half the citizens of the state hate his guts or are ashamed to have him as Premier.

Peanut Joh stays in power by what is known in political circles as a gerrymander which you get by dividing the place into electorates so cunningly that you can win every election with about a third of the votes.

A minority of electorates are constituted so that your opponents (in this case, the ALP) get almost all the votes; leaving the other electorates with a large majority of right-wing or swinging voters.

These latter electorates decide the result. And bingo! Get about 36 per cent of the total vote and 55 per cent of the vote in the latter electorates and you can rule forever.

The gerrymander makes a mockery of democracy. It is an old American and Qld custom. When Red Ted Theodore was Premier of Qld he decided to make a certainty of Labor staying in office by gerrymandering the seats.

Later, Sir Joh turned the gerrymander around.

Many years ago, I said that the typical Australian had come traditionally from Qld, especially north of Brisbane.

*The Sydney Bulletin* – then edited by Peter Coleman – published photos of me and Peanut Joh side-by-side with my quote below.

Of course, that's not what I meant: Joh Bjelke-Petersen lives north of Brisbane but he bears no resemblance to your typical Australian – it's like comparing a whorehouse madam to a nun.

North Queenslanders have a good track record as the typical Australians: they are battlers, they have an ironic sense of humour, they've worked hard all their lives and on their territory the great struggles of Australian history – except Eureka – have been fought out.

And the radical working class movement is stronger there than in the south. And you can include Brisbane in this: take the SEQEB strikers and their supporters, and men and women like Ted and Eva Bacon, the late Bill Sutton – genius of the short story – Jack Henry, Jean Devanny, Senator George Georges . . . I could fill a whole issue of *People* with names of Qld battlers.

Go back into history and you'll find Qld to the fore in the fight for democracy and justice.

The great shearers' and maritime strikes of 1891 reached their highest peak of courage in Qld. At Barcaldine, armed shearers gathered to make a last-ditch stand.

At that time, Henry Lawson himself lived in Brisbane, and he visited the shearers' camp at Barcaldine a week or two before the armed battle.

Henry worked for the *Boomerang* and ran a weekly column, *Country Crumbs.* He also wrote for *The Worker*, which was edited by William Lane.

Returning to Brisbane from Barcaldine, Lawson wrote and published his famous poem *Freedom on the Wallaby*, which concludes:

So we must fly the rebel flag,
As others did before us,
And we must sing a rebel song,
And join in rebel chorus.
We'll make the tyrants feel the sting
Of those that they would throttle,
And they needn't say the fault is ours
If blood should stain the wattle.

A conservative politician named Brentnal quoted those lines in the Qld parliament – and proposed that Lawson be charged with treason.

After the defeats of 1891-92, *The Worker* was banned and the *Boomerang* went broke.

William Lane decided to build a communist colony, the first in the world. He could not get land in Australia so ended up taking a ship, 'The Royal Tar', full of utopian communists – including Mary Gilmore – to Paraguay.

The vast majority of these brave, if misguided, pioneer socialists were Queenslanders!

Then there was the Parramatta Park (Cairns) riot of 1932, a page torn out of the Australian history books, about which I have written.

So let us kick this habit of tarring all Queenslanders with the same brush as Bjelke-Petersen and his clique. Only a minority support him.

And Peanut Joh has not studied Qld history. And, as Goethe (I think) said: "He who does not study history is doomed to relive it."

Watch yourself, Peanut Joh.

# *Hardyarn*

I told Truthful Jones in the Carringbush Hotel about my theory of the two Qlds.

"You're right," Truthful said. "And there's another thing. A big percentage of those who vote for Joh weren't born in Qld."

"How do you mean?"

"The place is full of bottom of the harbour cheats, developers, abandoned wives of millionaires, drug peddlers, yuppies and other wealthy sun-worshippers. Must be hundreds of thousands of them up there – and they all vote for Joh."

"Yeh, it's a bloody disgrace with so much poverty in the country."

"I'm all for it actually . . ."

"What? I don't believe it!"

"Yeh, y'see, Qld has the highest percentage of fatal skin cancer in the world. So the rich bludgers and bitches going north is a form of culling, when you come to think of it."

"Have another drink and develop your theme."

Truthful looked at his watch: "Sorry, got to go to a meeting of the Coalition for the Judicious Culling of the Human Species.

"I'll move a motion that we put an ad in the trendy press telling all their readers to spend the rest of their lives in Qld. See you later."

# Truthful Jones' Idea – Cull Others Before They Cull You

Truthful Jones is a great yarn spinner – as great as Bill Harney, Tom Hardy, Walkie-Talkie Walker, Bill Borker or even Tall-tale Tex Tyrrell – he is also something of a philosopher, in an ironic sort of a way.

His theory of the idle poor will be published later in the year. Now, he has a new theory (or so he told me in the Carringbush Hotel the other day).

"You still a member of the Coalition Against Poverty and Unemployment?" Truthful Jones asked me.

"Yeh." I replied.

"Well, I'm forming another coalition. I'll join yours if you'll join mine."

"Sorry, I replied. "Last year the coalition took up half my time. This year I'll have to do less detail. It's on its feet now and I must get on with my writing, which includes a book, a film and a stage play."

"Well, you could just lend your name to my coalition as a patron. It'll read well on the letterhead," Truthful said, licking his lips.

Taking the hint, I said: "Have another drink and tell me about the other patrons you have in mind."

"I'll force one down, just to be sociable," Truthful replied.

"Well, the patrons already include no less a personage than Dooley Franks from Parramatta – and Chrissie Flannery, the old Rent-a-Kill himself."

"But Flannery is dead, isn't he?"

"Yeh, a very untimely demise. He would've been a handy man on the technical side of my coalition," Truthful replied sipping his beer, with that enigmatic smile which means he's up to verbal mischief.

"What the hell kind of coalition have you got in mind?" I asked with a laugh of mock horror.

The laugh was on the other side of my face when Truthful replied, keeping a straight face: "The Coalition for the Judicious Culling of the Human Species."

"I hope you're joking," I commented. "You've got to be bloody joking!"

"Me joking?" Truthful said. "You know I never joke. My coalition will do more good more quickly than your CAPU."

"How do you make that out?"

"Well," Truthful said, draining his glass to signal he was in a yarning-drinking mood.

"Take the parking fines you're always on about: some people pay them, some cut them out in jail, some don't pay them and pray the cops are so sick of hounding petty civil offenders instead of catching the Mr Bigs that they won't try too hard on parking fines."

"So?" I asked, ordering another drink.

"So, you cull out parking attendants."

"Cull them out?"

"Yeh, you encourage them to go on strike, make their lives miserable, or simply cull a few." Truthful was getting warmed up. "My theory is this: the human species is like a bed of flower seedlings, or a patch of young vegetable plants; if the garden is to flourish, the seedling beds must be culled out from time to time."

"Well," I said, entering the spirit of his awful running joke, "I must admit the theory has general validity in science and Brown Bombers would be as good a place as any to start – if you insist on forming this coalition."

"When one species grows too quickly, other species, in this case motorists, are endangered. Get the drift?" Truthful continued.

"My committee is open to suggestions for culling – tell the people who read *People* to send in culling proposals to the editor, the man with the white-handled pocket knife. Any ideas yourself?"

"Well, you could do worse than getting stuck into process servers, debt collectors and repo men," I said with a nervous laugh.

"An excellent suggestion," Truthful replied. "We would get much public support for that. With the economy in bad shape, nearly every battler is in debt."

He raised his right forefinger in mock righteousness: "We must cull mainly the secret enemies of the people, like tax collectors and ASIO agents."

His jest made me uneasy. "You could cull the odd yarn spinner."

"No way," Truthful responded. "we're an endangered species. The coalition will never cull endangered species."

"Have you drawn up articles of association?" I asked.

"Yeh, and elected office-bearers," Truthful said. "I'm treasurer, needless to say. And our constitution permits all financial members to make suggestions for culling.

"One suggested weights and measures inspectors, because they fine people, who sell rulers measured by the inch instead of centimetres, but the committee voted that the suggestion was trivial.

"Another proposed dictators and nominated Marcos for the culling axe."

"Not a bad suggestion. But ours is an Aussie coalition and we ain't got any dictators here although, admittedly, we got more would-be dictators per square mile than any country on earth.

"P'raps the membership of the Melbourne Club could be culled down to reasonable proportions – especially if they keep refusing membership to Jews, women, and black fellows."

"What about politicians?" I asked.

"Well, they're often threatened, though not a threatened species," Truthful said.

"But seeing as Bob Hawke has increased their number in Canberra, and Nifty says he's going to bring more into the NSW parliament; yes, we'll have to consider some judicious culling in the parliamentary sphere, all right."

"You'd have to be careful to be even handed, an equal number for each party." I said. "Have another beer."

"Thanks, but no thanks. Must be off or I'll be late for the monthly meeting of the Coalition for the Judicious Culling of the Human Species. Want to come along?"

"No, I'll stick to CAPU; it's slower but safer."

"You'll be sorry. We're planning our first culling job tonight."

As Truthful neared the door, I called: "Who are you going to cull?"

"Heroin importers," Truthful replied. He doffed his hat and was gone.

# *Hardy*arn

Truthful's definition of a Philippines election: "President Marcos has no children, only one wife – but five thousand pregnant ballot boxes."

# How To Pick the Winner

The ambition of the vast majority of Australians is to pick the winner of the Melbourne Cup.

Having consulted my turf adviser, known as Carringbush Man because he's the most eccentric person living in Collingwood, I am in a position to let *PEOPLE* readers into the know about several secret systems, all of which, given the right conditions, Carringbush Man says will surely select the winner of the Melbourne Cup.

Before revealing these secrets, however, as an historian of note, I must make some philosophical comments about this remarkable horse race which, at about 2.40pm on the first Tuesday in November, renders the whole nation silent, except the race commentators; but fortunately, including the politicians.

The Melbourne Cup is a remarkable event for more than one reason; apart from being the only horse race in the world for which a public holiday is declared, it is a ritual even more sacred to Australians than football and cricket – and telling yarns.

Before the Melbourne Cup was invented, the ambition of the vast majority of Australians was to own a pub (I knew a fellow tramp one time who almost screwed his way into a pub). But these days pubs aren't worth the trouble, what with poker machine clubs, brewery ownership and falling clientele through the action of the narrow-minded bureaucracy in introducing the breathalyser test.

The only man I ever knew who could prove that he not only did not want to back the winner of the Melbourne Cup – he didn't even want to own it – was a man named Dederang Dick, who owned and trained a few horses in that lush Victorian farming district.

Dederang Dick, like most horse trainers, looked like a horse and treated his horses better than his wife. If his wife became seriously ill, he gave her two Aspros and a hot lemon drink. If one of his horses showed the slightest sign of being sick, he called in an expensive veterinary surgeon and sat up all night to give succour to the ailing animal.

Dederang Dick's main aim in life was to win the Dederang Cup, which was held annually because there was only one race meeting a year in the district at the time I speak of.

After years of attempting to achieve this laudable aim, he came to the not unreasonable conclusion that the other horses were either ring-ins or, more likely city horses who had been given a speed-up dope.

So, he went to the local chemist, explained the situation and asked the chemist to make a "sting" to use on his horse in the forthcoming Dederang Cup. The chemist agreed reluctantly, only after Dederang Dick had pointed out that his family had lived in the district before the Man from Snowy River, and that he employed six otherwise un-employable people. The chemist asserted that the dope would not show up in a swab, and made it up in lumps of sugar.

At the track on Dederang Cup day, Dick gave the horse three lumps instead of one, just to make sure.

At the vital moment, a city steward who had been skulking behind a tree asked Dederang Dick: "What did you administer to that animal?"

Dederang Dick replied: "Only a few harmless lumps of sugar, Your Worship!" The steward, cunning like the lot of them, said: "If it's so harmless, let me see YOU eat a lump of it."

Dederang Dick immediately obliged by chewing a lump of the sugar and stuffing one into the mouth of the city steward, remarking: "So harmless it wouldn't even hurt a steward."

As he legged the jock up, Dederang Dick muttered: "This is a certainty! Take it to the front – and if you hear anything coming behind yer, don't worry – it'll be me or the city steward!"

The horse duly won by 10 lengths and, soon after the race a well-known city trainer approached Dederang Dick.

"That's a good staying type of horse you've got there," said the smart city trainer. "If you give it to me to train, I could win the Melbourne Cup with it."

Dederang Dick exclaimed: "You must thing I'm a mug – you win the Melbourne Cup with it and it'll get 10 stone in next year's Dederang Cup!" Obviously, Dederang Dick was a man without true Australian ambition.

I myself once actually owned a winner of the Melbourne Cup. I bought it in a Calcutta Sweep at the Fisho's club in Manly at a Calcutta night. (The origin of the word Calcutta is unknown, but this is yet another obscure Australian ritual rivalling the chook raffle.) The horse was by Lanesborough and, if I remember correctly, was called Piping Lane – and it duly shit in. I was very upset after the Cup when I came to pick up my horse and they wouldn't give it to me.

I've picked more than one winner of the Melbourne Cup over the years, including Kiwi. Actually, it was the Countess of Carringbush who picked it (her name is Robyn, and they call her the Countess because she's a terrific bird).

As usual on the first Monday in November, me and Carringbush Man sat up all night studying the form for the Cup and rating the horses. Just after dawn, the Countess herself got out of bed and asked what we'd been doing sitting up all night.

When told, she said: "You could've saved yourself the trouble. I know what's going to win the Cup. I was in the hairdresser's in Smith Street yesterday and a lady strapper told me that Kiwi was a certainty."

Carringbush Man tore up all our facts and figures, because he remembered that the Countess had picked up a winner in the Smith Street hairdresser's every time she'd had her hair done.

Kiwi duly came from last to first, and the Countess of Carringbush collected all our bets, because me and Carringbush Man were a bit on the pissed side, and she did not trust us not to get underpaid.

Trouble was, being a Sydneysider, she got off the racecourse train at the wrong station and it took Carringbush Man three days to find her.

Having set the matter in context, I propose now to tell you several methods of picking the winner of the Melbourne Cup.

1. Back the three placegetters in the LKS Mackinnon Stakes, the Moonee Valley Gold Cup and the Caulfield Cup, provided they have won a race of at least a mile and a half.

2. Study the list of horses tipped by the radio and newspaper forecasters, and back those neddies whose names are NOT on the list.

3. Get to know Carringbush Man who, although as mad as an Alice Springs snake, is quite a good form analyst. His secret is that he can read pepper pods in a glass bowl and forecast future events therein. (He picked the winner of the Moe Cup by this method in 1973).

4. Better still, get to know his sheila, the Countess of Carringbush; she's got glistening white teeth and jet black hair; and she dresses with style, although she rather spoils the effect after a few drinks by going over on her ankles in high-heeled shoes.

They lurk outside the Carringbush Hair Salon, in Smith Street, Collingwood, and wait for her to come out, having spoken to the lady strappers who regularly patronise this distinguished establishment.

She's quite approachable, is the old Countess, but you have to pitch your tone of voice and language according to the mood she's in: when on a "high" she speaks in a posh, Cambridge-like voice; when on a "down", she speaks like a Dubbo meatworker. Your linguistic alertness will pay off; she'll have the Cup winner, for sure.

5. This factor you can't ignore: Carringbush Man rang up when I was writing this treatise, to inform me that he has read in his pepper pods that this year's Cup will be won by a New Zealand-bred five years or older, carrying 55.5kg or less.

Well, there it is, and don't go ringing up the editor if you don't back the winner. There are two reasons for this humble request: if you haven't backed the winner, it'll be because you haven't understood the simple systems I have outlined above; and the other reasons is that I've got a bloody living to earn, and I'm hoping to sell the odd article to *PEOPLE*, enlightening its readers on other vital subjects.

# Dead Horse

I thought I'd kicked the yarn-spinning habit but there I was on the Murwillumbah Racetrack, the Billinudgel Hotel, and other posh establishments telling yarns about every subject under the Southern Cross and I discovered a strange thing about Australian yarns: they're mostly about men and told from the man's angle. Of course, there are historical reasons for this: the traditional yarns were told by men where there were no women and developed in the men-only bars at pubs.

In recent years, however, some excellent women comics have been telling yarns from the women's point of view: Sue Ingleton, Geraldine Doyle, Julie Whitehead and Tammy. There are others and some of them are as Rude as Rodney (God bless their feminist hearts).

Now, as some of my best friends are feminists, even separatists, I decided to take the laudible precaution of introducing women characters into the series. In this I was aided and abetted by Irina Dunn and the greatest character of them all, Lyn Dennestein, although Lyn rather spoiled my day at the races by slamming the tote window shut, saying: "Sorry, Truthful, they've jumped." Needless to say, the horse won.

I used my alter-ego, Truthful Jones (some of you are old enough to remember *Would You Believe*) to tell some of the yarns and do battle with a character I created called Liz Foster, a feminist from way back.

I must admit that I sometimes cry out "what the hell am I doing here?" Telling yarns to the locals in the Billinudgel Hotel and not knowing whether their peals of laughter were a compliment to the jokes or part of the unfailing desire of the average Australian battler to get his head on the Idiot Box.

Truthful Jones is not an Ocker or, perhaps, he is rather the real Ocker, the Australian battler who knows he can't win but he has to battle and takes a sceptical, ironic view of the human condition and cuts the toffs and rich bludgers and bitches down to size.

Here's another of the yarns that won me the Yarn Teller of the Year award:

An old farmer is driving along the Pacific Highway near St Ives when his horse takes it in its head to drop dead. And there he is with a dead horse and a cart full of milk and pumpkins in the middle of the road.

Needless to say, hundreds of cars drive past – until who should come along in a red sports car but an elegant lady who actually stops with a sympathetic air.

"Me 'orse is dead and I can't shift it or the cart orf the road," the farmer wails.

To his amazement, the good lady takes a tow rope from the boot of the car, secures the horse and drags it off the road. Then she helps the farmer to drag the cart.

He is utterly bewitched – then somewhat amazed when the good lady says: "I will give you $500 for your horse!"

"But it's 13 years old – and it's dead as well."

"It doesn't matter, I will give you $500 for it if you will help me get it to my house."

Now the farmer thinks that he's got a nut on his hands but the elegant lady proceeds to tie the other end of the tow rope to the back bumper bar and open the door for the farmer to get into her car.

By the time they get to the front of the double storey mansion in St Ives they are on first name terms – Jolly Jack and Genial Glenda.

Glenda goes to the garage and comes back with an axe and a crowbar, passes the axe to Jolly Jack and proceeds to get stuck into one of the gateposts with the crowbar.

By now Jolly Jack is a bit on the nervous side, to say the least, but he bashes down the other gatepost with the axe. Glenda then unties the tow rope and begins to drag the horse through the gate.

"Can I have me $500 now?" Genial Glenda assures him that he would get his $500 after he helps her get the horse into the house.

191

They do about $10,000 worth of damage getting the horse through the front door and Jolly Jack gets a dose of the jitters. "You can 'ave me 'orse for nothin'. It's 13 years old anyway."

Glenial Glenda said: "A deal is a deal, Jack. When we get the horse up that spiral staircase you can have your money."

That spiral staircase was worth $20,000 — that is until Genial Glenda and Jolly Jack wreck it with the crowbar and the axe. They drag the horse up on to the landing, into the bathroom and, after wrecking the door and the screen, into the bath.

Downstairs again, Jack asks for his 500 bucks just once more and Glenda said: "First, we are going to have a whisky. I'm married to the greatest bloody know-all that ever God put breath in. He is a rich broker but he has got the brain of a baboon, yet he has to have the last word about everything. I've been married to him for 15 years, brought up two kids, went back to university and became a Master of Arts — but he still doesn't listen to a word I say and has the last word on every subject. In five minutes he'll come out and go to the toilet in the bathroom."

They sip their whisky and wait. And sure enough the baboon broker goes into the bathroom. Then he comes to the top of the stairs and calls out: "Glenda! There's a horse in the bath!" and Glenda says with gusto and glee: "Tell me something I don't bloody know." If feminists don't love that yarn — I give up.

# Hold Your Horses!
# Join the Punters' Union

Your Aussie battler has traditionally been union conscious.

Australia has more unions than you could poke a stick at. Yet, dear people who read *People*, the largest section of the exploited population of this country hasn't got a union.

And who are they? The punters, that's who!

It has been estimated by no less of an authority than Truthful Jones that 90 per cent of the Australian community gamble, even if only on the occasional Scratchit ticket or the Melbourne Cup.

More than 50 per cent of the population are regular betters on four-legged animals (for that read, dogs, galloping and trotting horses – the old Truthful reckons they stick to the four-legged lottery because their sceptical nature leads them not to bet on anything that can talk).

Never was so much money ripped off by so few (to wit: the bookmakers and the TAB) from so many in history.

The need for a Punters' Union has often crossed between the beer glasses of me and the old Truthful. My resolve to propose that one be formed was triggered recently when I telephoned a bet on a Melbourne race to the TAB only to have it placed on a Sydney race.(Never, but never, make a telephone bet without checking the name of the horse or horses!)

Upon discovering with horror that my account was light on I rang the TAB, only to be told that they had ceased only the day before to spot-check the tapes kept for the purpose of deciding disputed bets.

A supervisor informed me of this strange intelligence in a haughty voice and said that I must write a letter, upon receipt of which a form would be sent to me to fill in giving the exact time of the bet or bets.

I received – instead of the abovementioned form – a letter from an individual who signed himself L. Gruit, telephone betting controller (may all our gods protect us from such breeds!) "Our records indicate that you have changed your address from that which is registered with Phone Tab . . . to ensure the protection of your account, the TAB requires that change of address notification be in writing.

"It will therefore be appreciated if you would complete the instruction form hereunder and return it in the postage paid envelope provided.

"On receipt of this instruction, your earlier accounts statement request will be actioned."

Can you believe it? No mention of the fact that the TAB owed me about 300 nicker, only a reprimand for not having informed the TAB in writing of my change of address.

I still haven't got the money; maybe it will arrive in time for me to buy some Christmas presents.

Soon after the receipt of the above monstrous missive, I bumped into Truthful Jones and Bronte Sam (the old Sam is a dog punter). So I show 'em the bloody letter from the stinking TAB, don't I?

And soon we formed ourselves into a convening committee for the purpose of setting up an Australia-wide Union of Punters.

We discussed basic principles and planned conferences at Easter (no, not in a telephone box, smart arse), to be held if possible in the Carringbush Hotel, Melbourne, and the Harold Park Hotel, Sydney.

We chose Easter because not even Jesus Christ himself was crucified as badly as the average punter is in this country – and it only happened to him once. It is proposed:

1. That all persons who gamble on horses or dogs be invited to join the Punters' Union.

2. That the Punters' Union be incorporated and registered with full rights before the Arbitration Commission of Australia.

3. That a log of claims be drawn up and submitted first to the TAB and then all associations of bookmakers.

4. That all members or intending members of the

abovementioned union have the right to submit claims to be put in this log.

5. Self evident demands for the log shall include:–

(a) All gambling losses to be made tax deductible. (This is reasonable when it is considered that many of the biggest gamblers on the stock exchange pay no tax at all.)

(b) That pensioners and other disadvantaged people be picked up in buses and driven to the TAB or the racetrack.

(c) That the Wentworth Park Dog Track be instructed to complete the work on the new grandstand which has been going on for six years, and reduce its entrance fee from $5 to $3 to bring it in line with Victorian dog tracks.

(d) At the suggestion of Brother Jones, the union conveners are considering requesting that the TAB pay out on: winners; and horses that tried to win but the jockeys wouldn't let them. (This proposal will be referred to the federal executive to be elected at Easter.)

(e) In the unlikely event of a jockey winning on three consecutive odds-on favourites, he should be knighted on the spot in front of the members stand; that a representative of the Queen be present at all meetings for this purpose; and smelling salts be on issue to help resuscitate punters suffering from shock.

We, the undersigned, hereby request that punters throughout the Great South Land forward suggestions and express their interest in joining the proposed Punters' Union.

Letters should be sent to Frank Hardy care of *PEOPLE* magazine, 57 Regent St., Chippendale, 2008. Frank J. Hardy, author; Truthful Jones, yarn spinner; Bronte Sam, barker better.

P.S. All correspondence will be replied to: F.H.

# *Hardyarn*

A cheeky jockey arrived at the pearly gates.

St Peter told him: "Sorry, jockeys find it hard to get in here." When the jockey argued the point, St Peter said: "Well, if you've done anything outstanding, like riding the winner of a Melbourne Cup, I might be able to let you in."

"Well," replied the jockey. "I pulled up a 5-1 on favourite in a weight for age race at Randwick. When the crowd booed, I threw my cap over the fence at them; and when the chief steward said there was going to be an enquiry, I told him to get stuffed as I was too busy."

"When did you do that?" asked St Peter.

"About 30 seconds ago," replied the cheeky jockey.

# Seditious 'n' Speechless in Newcastle

I spent the Australia Day weekend in Newcastle, a city I've loved since Adam was a lad.

The Countess of Carringbush is still up there with her Lady in Waiting – Lady Di, formerly of the Maitland Ladies Cricket Team (no prizes for guessing what she's waiting for!)

The Countess also knows a big blonde named Deslie Shakespeare who was doing the PR for the Newcastle Hunter Regional Australia Day celebrations (being Newcastle, it lasted a whole week).

So Deslie rings me up and says the Countess has recommended me for the role of VIP guest of the Australia Day week. I accepted, needless to say; a week's free bed and breakfast at the Novocastrian – and all those great beaches from Nobby's Head to Belmont.

Deslie used to work for John Laws.

She also appeared for a while on *Beauty and the Beast*.

I autographed copies of *The Loser Now Will Be Later To Win* at Arthur Warner's bookshop, and did some radio and press interviews.

Early in the week there was this champagne breakfast. Such breakfasts, for me, have two drawbacks: you have to get up at the crack of dawn – and I hate champagne.

I wanted to put Australia Day in its correct context: (our original inhabitants had been here for about 80,000 years before the Anglo-Saxon-Celts came as the first migrants) to answer Professor Geoffrey Blainey, who had said that Australia gave minorities too many rights and implied that Australia Day should be a kind of Anglo-Saxon-Celt celebration.

I sprinkled Australian ironic jokes amongst the political comment.

The breakfast went off good too. A girl called Helen said she liked me because I was real. It was unreal!

Then bronzed Barbara made my day by saying she admired the stand I had taken and all the writing I'd done over the years.

During the week, I looked up old friends. Then came the big dinner with 500 guests. I turn up with the Countess of Carringbush to find at the main table an archbishop, two navy captains, one lieutenant-commander, the local ALP member, Alan Morris – and Bernard King!

Then Deslie – the big blonde – and her friend, Adele, take the stage and start handing out the prizes, including the sportsman of the year, which went to a weightlifter who looked as if he weighed 35kg wringing wet in an army overcoat with house bricks in the pocket. Turned out to be an Olympic medal winner.

Then Adele calls me to the stage. She makes a dainty speech and hands me a mounted map of Australia, carved in wood.

I read the inscription: "Newcastle Hunter Regional Australia Day council – Famous Australian Award. Let it be known that we honour Frank Hardy Our Most Australian Australia. Pres. H. Chambers."

Speechless for the first time in me life, I was, but managed to mumble something about never winning anything before, not even a $2 prize in the Scratchit Lottery, except a TV Logie the same year as my sister Mary, who won seven. Can't remember a word of my speech.

Arriving back in Sydney, I placed the Map of Australia in a prominent spot on the book case – only to discover that Tasmania had been left off it.

Poor old Tassie! If someone will send me a small drawing of it, I'll have it carved in wood and tagged on to my Famous Australian Award.

Here's the yarn that did the trick at the Newcastle Australia Day champagne breakfast (I drank beer):

# *Hardy*arn

Pat migrated to Australia for a year. When he arrived back in Dublin his mate, Mick, said to him:

"And how was it, Pat, old mate, what koind of people are these Aussies after all?"

"The Australians," says Pat, "are the most wonderful people in all the woide world."

"And that's the simple truth.

"With the Australians it's a case of share and share aloike. It's what they call mateship.

"The stranger comes to them and they make him welcome the loike of the prodigal son returning in the Bible and him not a son at all nor any relative even.

"And, if you have no money and the Aussie has two dollars he'll give you one and never ask for it back.

"Ah, they're darlin' people, the only true Christians left in the world.

"If you're a fugitive on the run, the Aussie will hoide you. And no matter who you are, the Australian will give you a fair go."

"Pat," Mick says, "they must be marvellous people, the Australians, and no mistake."

"It's loike I'm tellin' yer, says Pat, "they're the most wonderful people in all the world. When you've got a hangover, the Aussie will offer you a drink to loiven you up. What he calls the hair of the dog that bit you.

"Ah, they're people after me own heart. Do you know, if you have no home the Australian will invoite you to live in his home.

"And, may God stroike me dead if I tell a loie, if you have no wife, the Australian will let you share his wife."

Well, Pat's mate, Mick, says: "Pat, Oi'll admit from what you say Australians must be foine upstandin' people – but surely you found something in Australia you didn't loike?"

Pat hesitates for a moment, rubs his chin and says thoughtfully: "Well, Oi will admit Oi didn't get on too well with them white bastards out there."

# Darwin's Grog Gargler Sank Yank Morale in an Epic Binge

Tell me the most awful Australian yarn," I said to Truthful Jones in the Carringbush Hotel. "I've got the mother and father of a hangover, so speak softly. Went to my son Alan's birthday party last night. Have a hair-of-the-dog with me."

Truthful rubbed his chin: "You've got road-map eyes, a mouth like the bottom of a cocky's cage – and a stomach like an active volcano! Right?"

"Spot on!"

"Well, then, in your state of health, I can't tell you the most awful Australian yarn ever told – I'll tell you the second most awful. The yarn is called The World's Greatest Grog Gargler. He lived in Darwin. The official statistics show that they drink 254 litres a year in Darwin for every man, woman and child. The highest consumption in the world.

"One night in the Buffs Club, they were having a drinking competition to see who would wear the toaster's collar.

"The competitors are lined up to see who could down a pint the fastest, when this quiet, unassuming fella leaned on the bar and says: 'Do you mind if I have a go?'

"The president says: 'Be my guest.'

"This bloke grabs a 1.3 litre jug and downs it before any of the others drink a pint.

"He never took the jug from his lips but they could hear a strange gargling noise.

"The boys from the Buffs knew they had the new Darwin champ on their hands and nick-named him The Gargler.

"The reigning Darwin champ was a bloke at the Workers' Club, who drank 11 bottles in 12 hours.

"The only rule was a no-spew one – perhaps chunder is a better word.

"Well, a judge was appointed by the Licensed Victuallers Association to see fair play.

"The champ drank his first 11 in seven hours and seemed to be going easy when he chundered on the floor.

"He was disqualified under the no chunder rule.

"The Buffs Club decided to give The Gargler a go at the 12 bottle record.

"The Gargler – a very modest fella despite great achievements – says: 'I'd have to try meself out first to make sure I can do it – before you start betting on me.'

"From midnight, he drank a bottle an hour on the hour right through until midday without turning a hair."

"Did he eat anything?"

"No, and he never showed any signs of chundering either.

"The boys asked him: 'When will you start?'

"'No time like the present,' he says. 'I'll start now and go through till midnight.'

"The word spread through Darwin like rain in the wet season, and thousands of dollars were laid out in side wagers.

"Through the afternoon and into the night The Gargler gargled on and progress reports were spread by couriers: 'He's on his fifth bottle and going easy,' and 'He drinks a whole large bottle without taking it from his lips,' and 'He has a glass or two in between to quench his thirst.'"

"Have another drink. You're making me feel thirsty," I said.

"I'll force one down just to be sociable.

"Anyway, The Gargler drank the 12 bottles in 10 hours.

"No one in Darwin would try their skill against The Gargler after that, so a few of the lads took him down to Mt Isa.

"As soon as some of the Mt Isa mob started to boast about drinking, The Gargler modestly suggested a test of skill and endurance under LVA rules – no food, no chunder.

"Well, they cleaned up good money for a while until the local champion challenged The Gargler to a contest, drinking 1.3 litre jugs from a standing start for a side wager of $500."

"Here's your beer," I said. "The Gargler must have been a big powerful man to drink all that beer."

"It was a funny thing that; he was a little skinny fella.

"But he had two things in his favour that made him the world's greatest grog gargler: he had a pot belly and no epiglottis."

"What's an epiglottis?"

"It's the thing in your throat that makes drinking a slow process: he had no swaller, that's what it actually amounted to.

"Anyway, they stand with their hands behind their backs and a jug in front of each of them on the counter.

"The judge says 'Go'.

"The Gargler finished his before the other bloke got halfway. He drank it in 7.2 seconds flat according to the official timekeeper.

"Of course, they couldn't get a bet on in Mt Isa after that.

"So they head for Alice Springs, but word of The Gargler's exploits had spread ahead of them so they couldn't get any money on.

"Then The Gargler says: 'Tell you what I'll do, gentlemen. Just for a friendly game, I'll drink on me own against a team of eight. First to finish an 18 gallon keg is the winner.'

"No man in the world could beat an Alice team on his own.

"But The Gargler did it.

"Next they went to Tennant Creek and there the local champion says: 'I'll drink him under the table, if we mix the drinks.

"'We drink every drink on the shelf in order: beer, advocaat, cherry brandy, whiskey, and so on'.

"The Darwin mob had never seen The Gargler drink anything except beer.

"But they backed him and he won again.

"Then a very strange thing happened," Truthful said, pushing his empty glass towards Jill.

"You don't mean to say! Don't you call what you've been telling me strange?" I exclaimed.

"The Gargler decided to give up competitive drinking.

"'It's no use arguing with me,' he tells the mob from the Buffs. 'I'm retiring undefeated champ of Australia.

"'It's a matter of principle; we're taking people's money under false pretences.'"

"But I thought you said The Gargler eventually became world champion. Have another and get this awful yarn over with."

"The Gargler read in the paper that Yankee soldiers on leave from Vietnam were running what they claimed to be a world championship chug-a-lug in Hong Kong.

"A chug-a-lug is a drinking contest. The Yanks named it after a song recorded by Roger Miller: *The Chug-a-lug Song*. Anyway, The Gargler gets upset."

"Reckoned he should be world champion, I suppose."

"Not only that: he was crook on Yanks for some reason.

"People said his wife had run away with a Yankee provo on R & R from Vietnam.

"His Darwin backers had him on a plane for Hong Kong within a week.

"There were 50 entries for the championship and The Gargler didn't try too hard during the early rounds so they could get plenty of money on in the grand final.

"He drank off the big fat Yankee provo sergeant and the side bets ran into thousands of dollars.

"It was The Gargler's finest hour.

"He just kept one drink ahead while his mates kept laying bets like a two-up school.

"They drank beer and rye whiskey.

"The Gargler gradually drew further ahead until the Yank chundered over one of the judges and was disqualified."

"And so The Gargler became world champ. I don't believe a word of it," I said.

"The Yanks believe it, mate. The Gargler and his Darwin mates fleeced them for months.

"The American command issued a routine order-of-the-day about The Gargler: 'To all troops going on leave to Hong Kong. The steep fall in morale of combat troops in Vietnam is thought to be due to certain drinking contests being conducted.

"'Troops are advised not to enter into such contests with an Australian of dubious character who wears a drinking bib on which the words The Gargler are inscribed.

"'This man is believed to be an enemy agent endeavouring to undermine the health and morale of American troops.'"

"If that order was ever issued – which I doubt – it would put an end to The Gargler's career, fleecing our gallant allies," I says.

"It put an end to the war, as well. America pulled out of Vietnam because The Gargler had ruined the health of many of their crack combat troops," Truthful adds.

"That's the worst yarn I ever heard," I told Truthful.

"The second worst," he replied.

# *Hardy*arn

There I am parking my car beside a letter box in Kings Cross when a tall Brown Bomber with his cap on the back of his head tapped me on the shoulder.

"You can't park there, you mug!" he says through a huge walrus moustache that dangled above his mouth.

I'm about to abuse this strange example of a species I don't admire when he ripped off one side of his false moustache and whispered: "Don't tell a soul. I couldn't beat 'em so I joined 'em – and have been elected secretary of their union. I'm pulling them all out on strike next week!"

The Brown Bomber is none other than Truthful Jones.

So I shift my car – and Truthful yells out: "Cull! I say, cull!"

And, strike me dead if I tell a lie, they went on strike – and last I heard, they were still out. It's great! You can park anywhere. The Coalition for the Judicious Culling of the Human Species might be the right idea after all.

# Nursing Ills Still
# Need a Cure

Henry Lawson often complained, especially in the years from the turn of the century until his death in 1922, that he found it difficult to get his radical work published and that editors often gutted his work.

Lawson scholars have discovered many examples over the years.

A blatant piece of censorship was revealed by his grandniece, Olive Lawson, the granddaughter of Henry's brother, Peter, who was a composer and an organist.

Peter and Henry didn't get on, as the saying used to have it, so the subject of Henry was rarely raised with Peter's children. But Peter's grandchildren, plus Olive and her sister Sylvia, have become dedicated researchers of Lawson's life and work.

Olive concentrates on Lawson's life from 1906 to 1922, when he lived with Isabel Byers, whose loyalty and dedication kept him alive and writing longer than he would have done left to his own devices.

In the course of her research, Olive stumbled on a poem of Lawson's written in December 1902 or January 1903, called *The Old Head Nurse And The Young Marchioness*.

In some of Lawson's papers, released after the death of his daughter, Bertha, Olive Lawson found the original in Lawson's handwriting.

She checked it with The Landsdowne Press' *Complete Works of Henry Lawson,* edited by Cronin and Kiernan, and found no less than 28 lines had been deleted. These were deleted either by the editors of the *Complete Works* or by a sub-editor of *The Bulletin*, which published the poem while Lawson was still in hospital.

I must tell you why Uncle Harry went to hospital early in 1903.

The papers reported that he had fallen from a cliff at North Head, near Fairy Bower, Manly, and broken his leg.

Everyone assumed it was an accident but references by Lawson himself to the fall indicated it may have been a suicide attempt.

He had returned from London in 1902, the bailiffs had seized his furniture, his marriage had broken up and he was in a state of extreme depression.

Years later, writing of the incident with humour, Lawson said: "I tried to organise a funeral for myself."

While recuperating, Lawson wrote the long poem. After several verses describing the situation in the Sydney Hospital, Lawson turned to the subject of nurses:

I saw her first from a painful bed
Where I lay fresh from a fearful fall
With a broken leg and a broken head
In the accident ward of the hospital.

(The forced rhyme here and other blemishes in the poem, mark it as one of Lawson's lesser works – but he wrote it in bed with several stitches above his right eye as well as a broken leg.)

Twenty-eight lines were then deleted.

And it is significant that these lines referred to the bad working conditions and very low wages of the angels and slaves, as Lawson called the nurses.

Here are the missing lines – you may judge for yourself if their deletion was an act of censorship:

And speaking of nurses, now's my chance
to put in a word for the sisterhood
For they have little or no romance
The work is grand but their hearts are good.
(Tis sometimes better and sometimes worse)
But when the head is a Tartar, I know
Between the patients and that head nurse
The nurses have got a hard row to hoe.

They must be angel and slave in one,
Servant and student – and gritty? You bet,

and they cannot be sick till their work is done
And – you'd open your eyes at the wages they get
Oh, they must stick to it, early and late
They must be even a class apart
From human feelings like love and hate
(Though once I knew a nurse with a broken heart).

The same dull routine day after day,
the sores unsightly, the foetid breath
The shrivelled limbs and the faces grey
When the air is laden with sordid death.
The skip at the beck of a doctor lout,
the run for the screen – or whatever it be,
the same dull patients week in, week out
"Till our brains get rusty," a nurse told me.

The striving overmore to be kind
The doubt if a patient dies or lives –
"Because we never know what's behind
in the ignorance of the relatives."

Having made his point that wages were low and that doctors often acted like louts, the battered Lawson's poem continues:-

A tragedy fades like a fading scar
And marks of stitches above your eye
And I've seen much and I've travelled far
Since the day I wished they would let me die.

(Those words: "I wished they would let me die" also indicate a death wish.)

Space does not permit publication of the whole poem, but a study of those 28 missing lines, in my opinion, clearly indicates censorship.

That poem, of course, was written more than 80 years ago; like much of Lawson's work, it holds good for Australia today.

Nurses are still paid miserably low wages and their working conditions leave much to be desired – that is why we are faced with staff shortages in our hospitals.

I referred the 28 missing lines to Jenny Haines, of the Nurses Association.

Jenny responded: "Henry Lawson's words might have been written today.

"It would open many people's eyes if they knew that nurses receive only $324 a week for the first five years after training: that's $8.12 an hour.

After five years they receive only $9.35 an hour.

"These rates do not adequately reward them for the responsibility they take or the specialist knowledge they develop in giving good care to the sick and wounded."

Jenny Haines pointed out that the majority of nurses drop out after three to five years' work, because of the wages and conditions.

## *Hardyarn*

Years after his fall from the cliff at Manly, Lawson revealed that a fisherman named Sly had rescued him from the rocks.

Sly took him to Sydney Hospital. Lawson told poet-friend Edward Brady that he was "Sly by name and sly by nature" – because, when taking his leave of Henry at the hospital, Sly had said: "Better luck next time, Mr Lawson!"

Yes, better luck next time, Harry; that is to say, better luck with editors, publishers and academic critics than you had in your life.

# A Thousand Bucks Says There Isn't a Test Bowler Who Can Get Me Out

I n view of the fact, established below, that Australian cricket has reached such a state of crisis that it is in danger of disappearing as our greatest national game, we hereby challenge the Australian Cricket Board to:-

1. Produce any two bowlers from the present test team who can get author Frank Hardy out in (say) four overs.

2. Make a side wager of $1000 on the result.

3. Upon losing the bet, set up an independent committee of inquiry into the administration of cricket in this country; said committee's recommendations to save the game of cricket from extinction to be adopted by the Australian Cricket Board.

Signed: Frank Hardy, Witness: "Truthful" Jones.

There I was in the Carringbush Hotel agitating on the decline and pending fall of Australian cricket, when who should walk in but Truthful Jones.

"Been watching the cricket?" he asked, as though he could read my mind.

"Gave it away after the New Zealander tour debacle. The game's had it in this country."

Truthful tilted his hat on to the back of his head and licked his lips. I got niggly and said: "You're buying the drinks today, Truthful – and you're going to keep your trap shut. We're going to talk cricket."

Truthful got upset. "Listen mate, I pay for drinks – when I'm not telling yarns, and I only tell yarns for beer." He threw two gold dollars on the counter. "Two beers for two gentlemen please, Jill."

When Jill recovered from the shock she obliged, and I said: "Y'know, Truthful, I sat watching the last Australia-

New Zealand Test and I said to meself: 'I could get 50 out there, against either team, no risk.'"

"You were opening bat for Bensons Valley before you left school – but that was a bloody long time ago."

"It wouldn't be hard to make 50 against this present mob."

"Have another drink and get it off your chest. What's gone wrong?"

"Well," I said. "First came the commercialisation and the big money of the Chappell-Lillee-Marsh era and the win at any price philosophy, the under arm . . . the sledging . . . "

"Sledging?"

"Yeh, whispered insults to the batsman as the bowler ran up, racist remarks . . . but, as Clive Lloyd said, they called it gamesmanship, but they couldn't talk the Windies out of playing their own game."

"The greatest cricket team the game has seen, the Windies under Clive Lloyd."

"The Aussies under Don Bradman," I replied. "Imagine it: Ponsford, who made more double centuries than even Bradman, Stan McCabe, Bill O'Reilly, Clarrie Grimmet . . ."

"Not to mention Ray Lindwall and Keith Miller . . ."

"Next thing was Kerry Packer and the World Series Cricket. It split Australian cricket right down the middle; some signed up with Packer for the big money, others stayed in test cricket. Then The bloody cricket control board too over the one-day commercial cricket. It all resulted in Australian cricketers becoming schizophrenics . . ."

"So they're mental cases!"

"That's not what I meant. It's like Bille O'Reilly said: the batsmen play test matches the same as one day matches; and they play every shot with a cross bat; they've lost the art of forward and backward defence . . ."

Truthful looked at me with that two-faced ironic grin. "Well, you were the greatest defensive batsman in history. What was it – carried your bat against Darley, made 10 runs in seven hours?"

"Eleven. But I made 47 on the St Kilda Cricket Ground in country week – that's on the record in the Melbourne Sun."

210

"What about that century on the MCG?"

"You made that story up, and I began to believe it. I made only 87 against weak bowling." I hastened to change the subject. "But I did make a hundred for the Steyne Hotel, Manly, with only one pad on, but the bowlers and fieldsmen – and the scorer – were all drunk. And I made another on Clip-board Gerry's back yard pitch – with a tennis ball admittedly and very short boundaries.

"Next came the Kim Hughes South African tour, which proves just once again that most Australian cricketers would do anything for money – except learn the fundamentals of the game. And there's not enough facilities for junior and country cricket. Worst of all: in the old days, the experienced batsmen and bowlers in the test team would give hints to new players; these days they rarely hand on what knowledge they've got for fear they'll improve and cost them money by taking their places in the team."

Truthful rubbed his nose. "This is the first time I've seen you get upset about anything – except poverty – for five years." He ordered another beer. "Why don't you challenge the bastards?"

"How do you mean?"

"Well, Clip-board Gerry and Boo and Quinella Quentin have lost every bet they've made that they could get you out. Why don't you challenge the Australian bowlers that they couldn't get you out in (say) four overs under Test conditions."

"Jeez, Truthful, I haven't had a bat in me hands against a hard leather ball for 25 years."

"But you've got a perfect technique in forward and backward defence. You learned it from Don Bradman's photo book, when you were a kid. And the last season you played in Melbourne in 1950 you won the batting average for the Washingtons in Carnegie."

I glanced at Truthful to see if he was pulling my leg but his expression was, as usual, inscrutable. "Well," I admitted, "I did discuss some such challenge at the *People* Xmas party with the editor. We were pissed at the time – but he said he'd put up half the money for a $1000 side bet . . ."

"He of the white-handled pocket knife? He seems the kind of bloke who'd be as good as his word – even those spoken with an alcoholic tongue."

"I'll talk to him again when I get back to Sydney."

With that, Truthful Jones began to draft the challenge on the back of some Foster's Lager coasters.

# *Hardyarn*

Truthful Jones' definition of the ultimate optimist: "An Australian batsman applying the zinc cream before he goes to the wicket."

# There's No More Arty Umpire Around

Rules for the challenge match between Frank Hardy and the Australian XI:

1. Eleven Australian players shall take the field at the appointed time.

2. Two of these players, selected by the Australian Cricket Control Board shall bowl two overs each.

3. The said Frank Hardy shall have a batting partner and Keith Miller is suggested as the most suitable player. (Should the Australian bowlers fluke getting Miller out, this will not count and he may continue batting.)

4. No under arms shall be bowled.

5. Neutral umpires shall preside over the game. To ensure impartiality we propose that Arty McConkidale, of Bensons Valley, umpire at one end and an umpire chosen by the Australian Cricket Board of Control at the other.

6. A side wager of $1000 shall be made on the contest.

7. The bets shall be made in cash, no cheques or plastic money acccepted.

8. The money shall be lodged in a safe place in the custody of a reliable individual. Neville Wran is proposed (in the event of him being unavailable, his wife Jill could hold the money).

9. The loser of the bet (to wit – the Australian Cricket Board) shall divide the $1000 equally between a promising schoolboy cricketer and the Coalition Against Poverty and Unemployment.

10. The overs shall be bowled on the Melbourne or Sydney Cricket Ground.

11. In the meanwhile Frank Hardy shall be given access to the practice nets at the Sydney Cricket Ground.

Signed: "Truthful" Jones, Convenor of the Contest.

That day in the Carringbush Hotel, after Truthful drew up the challenge and the rules, he said: "I am about to tell a yarn so it's your shout."

He grinned ironically. "You, old mate, were a victim of the ravages of war: your promising career as a cricketer was interrupted when that bastard Hitler attacked Russia and the Japanese got stuck into Pearl Harbour.

"Some day someone should make a list of things ruined by war, including the careers of a lot of good cricketers. Take Ken Mueleman for instance, who was just at the peak of his form in 1940 when the war stopped cricket for five years. He played again after the war but never made it into the Australian team.

"And I reckon you would have got into the Victorian team if it hadn't been for the war – any man that can make a century with only one pad on has to be Shield material . . ."

"Thanks, here's your drink. I'd never have made it into the Victorian team, maybe Carringbush in the Districts . . ."

Truthful took a big swig of beer. "Sam Loxton would have been a victim of the war, too, but he kept in practice as you know. You must remember it; he was in an army camp at Bensons and getting out of practice. So he got in touch with the local cricket association.

"What about a friendly match?' he says. 'The competition's closed down,' they told him. 'All the cricketers are in the army.'

"Sam was determined. 'Couldn't you scratch a side together to play a team from the army camp?'

"Well, seeing it was Sam Loxton they did their best and fielded a team of old cricketers and soldiers on leave. A one-day game from 11 o'clock till six o'clock on a Saturday.

"I was in the army at the time, but I heard all about it," I said.

"I was bowling myself for Bensons at the time," continued Truthful. "Anyway, Bensons Valley won the toss and batted. Made about 150. Then the army team went in. Sam Loxton opened up himself. Wanted to get plenty of practice. He played for the strike. A good attacking batsman, Sam, not like the powderpuff crickets these days. By four o'clock, the army had passed the local team's score – but Sam wanted more practice.

"Now, at that time, the greatest cricket umpire Australia ever saw lived in Bensons Valley, name of Arty McConkidale. Knew the rule book off by heart.

"When he sat for his examinations for umpiring, Jack Ryder and all the experts tried to trick him but they weren't in the hunt. Got the highest pass ever in the exams. Would have been a test umpire only he was too fond of the gargle.

"The gargle has ruined many a good man. His father was a good umpire, too, but fond of the gargle, just like his son.

"They were umpiring this day. And they began to get terrible thirsty. Nearly a hundred in the shade it was.

"Anyway, by five o'clock, Sam Loxton's team was more than a hundred in front with only seven wickets down.

"So I said to Sam: 'Why don't you retire or declare the innings closed? The umpires are getting thirsty and the pubs shut at six.'

"'I need all the practice I can get,' Sam told me, 'and the game doesn't finish until six o'clock.'

"Well we managed to get two of the tail-enders out. Only one more wicket to fall. But Sam Loxton kept playing for the strike. Hitting us all over the ground, he was.

"I bowled him a short one outside the leg stump. He stepped right across and pulled it round to leg. The ball went like a rocket straight at Arty McConkidale, umpiring at square leg.

"He was standing there thinking, the pubs will be closed before they get him out. He had four cricket caps on his head, three white jumpers tied around his neck by the sleeves, a couple of watches on each wrist.

"The ball was coming straight at his face. He put his hands up and caught it . . .

"'How's that?' I appealed to Arty's father, who was umpiring at the bowler's end.

"He hesitated, licked his lips then raised his finger. 'Out' he said.

"And he lifted the bails and headed straight towards the pub. His son shook the caps, jumpers and watches into a heap on the grass and followed him. The two teams went, too, leaving Sam Loxton standing in the middle of the pitch wondering what rule he'd been given out under . . .

"First time a batsman was caught by the square leg umpire," Truthful concluded. "That's why I'm nominating Arty McConkidale as our umpire in the Challenge Match."

# *Hardyarn*

Years ago, a Lancashire Umpire had an eccentric habit of standing at the corner of the pitch when umpiring at the bowler's end, instead of behind the stumps.

One day, Peter Parfitt, the Yorkshire left-hander, came into bat. Peter saw where the umpire was standing and said: "Why don't you stand behind the stumps? You couldn't give a leg-before decision from there."

In the first over, Peter was rapped on the pads and given out leg-before in a very doubtful decision.

As Parfitt walked, the Lancashire umpire remarked: "Thought you said I couldn't give a leg-before decision from here."